Anybody's Bike Book

Tom Cuthbertson
Illustrated by Rick Morrall

TEN SPEED PRESS
Berkeley, California

1⊜

Ten Speed Press
Post Office Box 7123
Berkeley, California 94707
www.tenspeed.com

Distributed in Australia by Simon and Schuster Australia, in Canada by Ten Speed Press Canada, in New Zealand by Southern Publishers Group, in South Africa by Real Books, in Southeast Asia by Berkeley Books, and in the United Kingdom and Europe by Airlift Book Company.

Cover design by Fifth Street
Interior design by Jeff Brandenburg/ImageComp
Illustrations by Rick Morrall

Library of Congress Cataloging-in-Publication Data on file with the publisher.

ISBN 0-89815-996-2

First printing this edition, 1998
Printed in Canada

2 3 4 5 6 — 05 04 03 02 01

This book is dedicated to Dylan Dickie,
and to all new cyclists like him who
are learning to fix their bikes.

Contents

List of Illustrations vi

Introduction xi

Getting a Bike 1

1   **Getting Set to Ride and Repair** 9
    Rules of Thumb 9
    When and Where to Ride 14
    Quick Maintenance Check 14
    Tools and Other Stuff to Take 15

2   **Brakes** 29
    Hand Lever 32
    Brake Cables 38
    Brake Mechanism 46
    Coaster Brake 58

3   **Handlebars and Stem** 67

4   **Headset** 77

5   **Frame and Fork** 85

6   **Wheels and Tires** 93
    Tires 94
    Hubs 114
    Spokes and Rims 121

7   **Seat or Saddle and Seat Post** 135

8   **Power Train** 143

9   **Front Half of Power Train** 147
    Pedals 148
    Cranks 154
    Bottom Bracket 160
    Front Sprocket or Chainring 164

10 **Chain** 169

11 **Back Half of Power Train and Gear Changers** 179
    Rear Sprockets 179
    Gear Changers 185
    Control Lever or Grip 196
    Cable 203
    Front Changer 206
    Rear Changer 208

Postscript 213

Appendix: Vestiges 215

Index 221

List of Illustrations

Brakes

2-1 The Three Units of a Brake System, 31
2-2 Mountain Bike Brake Lever, 32
2-3 Aero Brake Lever, 33
2-4 Old Style Brake Lever, 33
2-5 Brake Cable and Ends, 38
2-6 Adjusting Sleeve, 40
2-7 Clean Cut and Burr in Housing End, 45
2-8 Cantilever Brake, 46
2-9 V-Brakes, 47
2-10 Side-pull or Caliper Brake, 48
2-11 Side-pull Mechanism, 50
2-12 Brake Shoe, 56
2-13 Coaster-Brake Hub, 61

Handlebars and Stem

3-1 Handlebars, 70
3-2 Top: Standard Stem; Bottom: Locknut Stem, 71
3-3 Straightening a Bent Drop Bar, 73
3-4 Drop-Bar Taping, 75

Headset

4-1 Threadless Headset, 79
4-2 Standard Headset, 80
4-3 Holding Fork in Headset, 83

Frame and Fork

5-1 Frame, 85
5-2 Fork, 87
5-3 Pulling Out the Front End, 89

Wheels and Tires

6-1 Wheel Parts, 93
6-2 Two Different Tire Valves, 96
6-3 Using Tire Irons, 99
6-4 Roughing up the Tube, 104
6-5 Applying the Patch, 105
6-6 Pushing the Tire Bead On, 107
6-7 Tightening Rear Wheel in Place, 110
6-8 Edge Test, 112
6-9 Pumping Up, 113
6-10 Hub, Exploded View, 116

6-11 Last-Ditch Wheel Straightening, 123
6-12 Squeezing a Blip, 126
6-13 Straightening a Minor Wobble, 128

Seat or Saddle and Seat Post

7-1 Clamp-top Seat Post, 136
7-2 The Seat, 138

Power Train

8-1 Power Train, 144

Front Half of Power Train

9-1 Top: Standard Type Pedal; Bottom Clipless Type Pedal, 149
9-2 Pedal, Exploded View, 150
9-3 Tightening and Loosening a Left-Hand Pedal, 152
9-4 Cotterless Crank, 155
9-5 Bottom Bracket, Exploded View, 161
9-6 Crank and Chainrings, 165
9-7 Bending a Tooth, 166

Chain

10-1 Master Link, 170
10-2 Two Different Chain Links, 174
10-3 Chain Tool Spreading Tight Link, 175
10-4 Chain Tool Driving Out Rivet, 176
10-5 Checking Chain Looseness, 177

Back Half of Power Train and Gear Changers

11-1 Chain Whip and Remover in Action, 182
11-2 Freewheel with Slots, 183
11-3 Changer Adjustment, 188
11-4 Rear Changer in High Gear, 193
11-5 Rear Changer, 195
11-6 Thumb Trigger, 197
11-7 Double Control Lever, 198
11-8 Tip (Bar End) Shifter, 198
11-9 Brake Lever Gear Control, 199
11-10 Down-Tube Control Lever, 200
11-11 Grip Shift, 200
11-12 Front Changer, 207
11-13 Rear Changer, 209

Please Note

Throughout this manual, (cl) means clockwise, and usually tightens a bolt or nut. (c-cl) means counterclockwise, and usually loosens.

The boxed symbols at the beginning of each new procedure indicate which type of bike is being discussed:

C Cruiser

R Road Bike

M Mountain Bike

Acknowledgments

Thank you Colleen, for all your support and love.
Thanks to all the folks who helped me put this book together, including:

Mark and Berri Michel and the Bicycle Trip gang of Steve Hess, Annie Kappl, Mike Ferrentino (writer of great BIKE articles), Luigi Puzziferro, Ben Capron, Judie Scalfano, Kurt Stephens, Adam Henderson, David Crum, Rick Hunter (maker of fine frames), Zac Cordell, Julene Mitchell, Eric Wilhelm, Ezra Manners, and Mark Hoffman.

Dennis Brady, Matt Kalastro, and the crew at Another Bike Shop.

John Brown of the Family Cycling Center.

Jim Langley of *Bicycling Magazine*.

The Wrecking Crew and editors at *Mountain Bike Action Magazine*.

Andrew Muir, Brian Raney, Stacey Campbell, Jeffrey Hing, Andy Schloss, Paul Sadoff, Diane Walker, Peter, Haase, Steve Hubbard, Bruce, Tim, and all the other mountain bikers who took those Friday rides with us.

Many thanks to these others who pitched in on earlier editions: Paul Schoellhamer, John Thess, Dan Nall, Roger, Marcia and Don Sands, Phil Shipley, Syd Joselyn, Johnny and Vic of Johnny's Bike Shop, Kathy Rose, Gary Macdonald, David Morrison, Kim Jacobs, Jim Houston, Laurie Karl Schmidtke, Billy Menchine, Pat and Nancy Heitkam, Michael Ray, Mark Jansen, Bryan Loehr, Gary Barnett, Jeff Jolin, Rick Gaytan, Brian Tailleur, Pete Lee, and Jack Taylor. Last but not least, thanks to Cory, my son and cycling soulmate.

Introduction

This is a book about fixing bikes. It tells a little bit about each of the parts on your bike, then tells you how to diagnose the problems with each part, and how to fix them.

For each problem described, I give two approaches for repairs. First, I tell you what to do if you're out on the trail or road, with only a few simple tools and fewer spare parts. Second, I tell you what to do when you're at home, with good tools and parts from your local bike shop.

There is a basic assumption behind both approaches. If something goes wrong with your bike, YOU CAN FIX IT! Even if you've never fixed a bike or anything else, you really can fix up all the problems described in this book. Some of the procedures are easier if you get a little help from a shop mechanic, but you can master even those tasks on your own, given time and patience.

Needless to say, this book can't cover every oddball repair for every obscure custom bike made. But there are procedures for almost all mountain bikes, road bikes, and cruisers. Each paragraph has a tag at the beginning that tells what kind of bike it covers. Even if I don't cover your exact type of bike, if you use your common sense, read the appropriate procedure, and think a bit, you can figure out a solution to your problem that will get you riding again.

All you really need is this book, a few simple tools, and your common sense. Ain't that grand? How many automobile owners can make that claim? Bikes are so simple and efficient. They are so good for our natural surroundings, too. Especially if we ride them with love and respect for those surroundings.

So go for it. But go lightly on mother nature, OK? She's an old friend of mine.

Getting a Bike

Before you buy a bicycle, think about what you are going to use it for. Then look at used bikes as well as new ones that will fit your needs. A well-cared-for used bike is one of the greatest re-cycles!

If all you want to do is ride around the neighborhood or noodle down to the store, all you need is a sturdy 1- or 5-speed bike. Even a rusty trashmo may do the trick; I have

such fond memories of my old balloon-tire bomber! If rusty-trusty bikes don't appeal to you, try one of the spiffy new versions of the classic fat-tire cruisers. You can even get restored balloon-tire bikes, but the prices are often as balloony as the tires. Keep fenders and a chainguard on your cruiser/trashmo if you live in a place where it rains. For family service, you can put a basket and a child seat on the bike and make it into a station wagon; sure, it'll be a heavy bike, but it'll work fine for errands.

For kids that are too big for a child seat, there are small 1-speed bikes; if your kid is just learning to ride, make sure you get a bike that's small enough so the munchkin can sit on the seat and reach the ground with both feet. That way, you can take the pedals off the thing and let your kid walk it around to get the feel of balancing. This works much better, in most cases, than a taller bike with training wheels.

For rambunctious kids who can ride well, there are BMX and stunt bikes that have one speed, 20- or 24-inch wheels, and light-but-strong components adapted from the larger racing bikes. Be cautious when buying such bikes. There is a lot of hype and peer pressure that tend to lead young

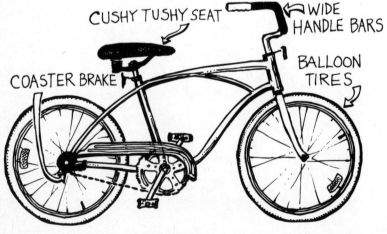

CUSHY TUSHY SEAT

WIDE HANDLE BARS

COASTER BRAKE

BALLOON TIRES

Cruiser

people to buy the faddish bike rather than the bike that works best for what they want to do. As a parent, I advise kids to get a sturdy, solid BMX bike from a reputable bike shop; it'll cost about twice as much as the bargain-store bikes, but it'll last MUCH longer and hold its value for trading up. If you get really fanatic about BMX racing or stunt riding, then you can work your way up to a bike with a super-light frame and wheels, and a super-heavy price tag. If you work your way up, you'll probably get the bike you really need, instead of one that's the fad of the day.

Back to the grown-ups. If you want to do more extensive riding in town, and maybe take an occasional jaunt on back-country trails, get a multispeed, wide-tire mountain bike. They were originally made for screaming down precipitous fire trails in Northern California, but people have found they are fun to ride just about anywhere. They combine some of the lightness and high-tech performance of road racing bikes with sturdy brakes and wheels, a comfy riding position, and the cushy wide tires from the old ballooners. There are also many hybrid bikes; some have more gears, some fewer, some have thinner wheels or beefier components, and some are designed to be more responsive than others. But on almost all of them, you sit up more than you do on the racey drop-bar road bikes, and you ride on wider tires.

The wide tires mean it doesn't hurt when you go over bumps, and they mean you don't get nearly as many flats when you go over sharp objects. These are both strong advantages for around-town riding, as well as riding out in the boonies.

The sit-up position is the biggest advantage, though. It means you feel comfy and more stable than you do on a bike with turned-down handlebars. It also means you are fighting a bit more wind resistance, so you can't go as fast

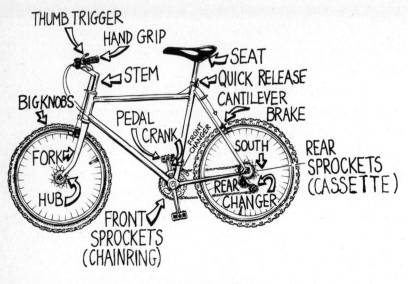

Mountain Bike

as a comparable rider on a road racing bike, but you can still move right along.

I enjoy the *feeling* of speed I get on a mountain bike; my head is up in the wind; my eyes are looking around me, taking in the scenery as it whooshes by. On the classic road bike, your head is bent way down in that low-wind-resistance position so you can go faster, but all you get to see is the spinning front wheel. Sure, it's spinning at the max speed, but who cares, after staring at it for an hour or two?

Speed is relative, after all. In galactic terms, we are all moving at a blinding pace toward oblivion. In more down-to-earth terms, no matter how hard we pedal *any* bicycle, we barely move in relation to passengers flying by in a jet. And yet, the jet passengers are just SITTING there, in a compartment that gives no sense of speed or motion at all. It's relatively boring. On the other hand, have you ever seen that great picture of Einstein, the mastermind of relativity, on a bicycle? He doesn't look like he's trying to attain the speed of light. Looks like he's riding relatively slowly, in fact. But he's GRINNING! Mountain bikes and their city-bred cousins are a good choice if you care relatively more about having fun, and relatively less about going fast.

Mountain bikes and hybrid bikes can have shock absorbing suspension for the front wheel, or for both the front and back wheels. Shocks dampen the bumps your bike goes over, but they add to the price and the weight of your bike. If they are really put to use on rugged terrain, they tend to wear out and require maintenance or expensive repairs. I think shocks are best suited to downhill racing experts, who really need the extra speed they make possible, and who can afford the necessary repairs. For folks who do most of their riding around town, shock absorbing suspension is unnecessary. If you like the whooshy feeling you get riding on shocks, fine. Just get a bike with shocks that are as light as possible, and that have a good reputation for reliability. There's no rule against enjoying that smooth ride going over potholes and curbs around town, or over the minor bumps along that gravel lane through the park.

Some of you may want to take longer road rides, though. For getting away from it all, for covering many paved miles in comfort and at speed, get a light (20- to 25-pound) multispeed road bike like the one below. Road bikes can be fitted with carrier racks and packs to carry anything from a spare tire to full camping gear and the kitchen sink, but remember, the less you carry on a light road bike, the more you enjoy its lovely *lightness*.

For cyclists who want to take day-, week-, or even month-long trips, there are touring bikes made to cover the miles comfortably, and carry all you need to take with you. Any sturdy, light (25- to 30-pound), well-made road bike with carrier eyelets (the little holes on the frame for mounting racks and fenders) can be used for touring, but bikes with specially designed frames and extra strong wheels and tires will make life on the road easier. Mountain bikes can be used for touring, but the sit-up position gets tiresome and painful after days in the saddle.

Of course, there are cyclists who like to race other cyclists. Ultra-light road and mountain bikes with space-age alloy components are made for racers who can afford their high costs. There are super little BMX racing bikes that are just as high-tech! For Olympic-style banked-track racers, there are fixed-gear bikes that weigh less than 15 pounds, and yet are strong enough to hold up under the strongest sprinters. Most of these bikes are too specialized for me to cover in this humble book.

There are also many specialty bikes other than those discussed above. If you want to get an unusual or very elegant machine, though, remember that you may have difficulty figuring out how to fix it, and replacement parts may be hard to find. For instance, if you want to ride a recumbent

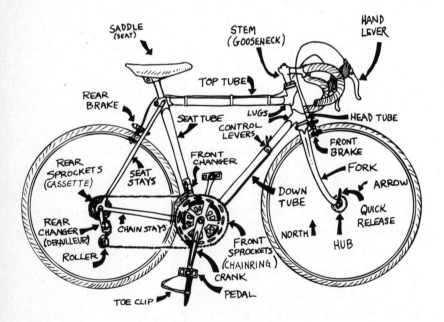

Road Bike

(one of those long, low bikes that you ride sitting down close to the ground), try to get one that has more or less standard bike components, rather than exotic custom parts that can't be fixed or replaced.

When you have decided what type of bike you want, shop around and see as many different brands as possible. Remember, as you compare bikes, that the *frame* is the most expensive and significant part. If you buy a bike with a good frame, you can make equipment changes to suit yourself without spending a lot of money. But if you buy a bike with a heavy, weak frame, you are stuck with it. For some specific suggestions and hints, see the "Frame" chapter.

The wheels and tires are almost as important as the frame. Get wheels that are strong enough to do what you want, and as *light* as possible. Sealed bearings make sense for mountain bikers who see a lot of dust or mud. There are lots of different tires for most types of bikes. In general, you want to buy tires that grip on the surfaces you ride over, and that resist punctures, but aren't any heavier than necessary. You road bikies, don't go for the super-light, tubular, or sew-up tires unless you are a road or track racer. For more info, see the "Wheels" chapter.

Take any bike you might buy on a test ride. First make sure the tires are pumped up and the seat is adjusted for your size. Then ride the bike up and down hills, around curves, over rough and smooth pavement. Ride fast, ride slow; try making quick little turns (on smooth dry pavement) to test out the steering. Be thorough. Get the feel of the bike. If it feels good, buy it; if not, don't. And don't be afraid to let the color of the bike influence your decision. If you like the color of your bike, you'll ride it more and care for it better. I *love* dark blue bikes, for instance. If you *love* bright red bikes, get a bright red one.

If you can't decide between two similar brands, ask politely if you can talk to the mechanics who assembled them, and find out which bike "went together easier." The bike that works well for the build-up mechanic will work well for you, most likely. If the dealer doesn't want you to distract the mechanic, respect the dealer's judgment.

Be decent to bike dealers, and you'll find they will usually be decent to you. That sounds silly, but I have worked in and been around bike shops for years, and I've been dismayed by the indecent behavior of some customers. I think the problem often stems from a combination of defensiveness and unrealistic expectations. So please, try to make the bike shopping experience a positive learning experience, and don't expect a new bike you buy from a shop to be absolutely perfect. Bicycles are made by humans. To err is human. Use this book and it will help you overcome the human element of error. Go through the *Quick Maintenance Check* with your new bike and read and follow the chapters on the parts referred to. That will familiarize you with your bike, and this book as well.

If you have trouble with a new bike, politely ask the shop people for help. Nine times out of ten, they will oblige— especially if the shop is the kind that offers a 30-day checkup with your new bike, to take care of those new-bike problems. The fact is, some of the problems you have with your new bike might be due to *your* newness to *it*. You are as human as the people who built the bike. It takes a while for a new rider and a new bike to get acquainted. Give your relationship with your bike a little time and patience; you will be well rewarded.

CHAPTER 1

Getting Set to Ride and Repair

To limit your troubles out on the trails and roads, learn a few Rules of Thumb about your bike and check its condition before you leave on a ride, then ride at sensible times, in sensible areas, and with a sense of your own limitations. That's all simple advice, but the type of advice we tend to forget. So here's a short collection of reminders about your bike and how to use it.

Rules of Thumb

1. In this book, "left side" means the left side of the bike when you are sitting on it facing forward. The same principle goes for "right side." Each paragraph of the book has a tag that lets you know what kind of bike it's about: mountain bike, road bike, or cruiser. If you have a hybrid bike, most of the parts on it are like mountain-bike parts, so read those **M** paragraphs to solve your problems.

2. To shift your bike into a LOWER gear, you have to move the right-hand gear control the hard direction (against resistance) and the left-hand gear control the easy direction (no resistance). To shift your bike into a HIGHER gear, you have to move the right-hand gear control the easy direction and the left-hand gear control the hard direction. This rule works no matter what kind of lever, ratchet, or twisting grip your bike has for controlling the gears. The only exceptions occur in rare gear systems with counter-sprung front or rear changers. For more hints on gear shifting, see page 186.

3. On most bolts, nuts, and other threaded parts, clockwise (cl) tightens, and counterclockwise (c-cl) loosens. NOTE THESE EXCEPTIONS: left pedals and some right-side bottom-bracket parts. They have left-handed threads, bless their twisted souls; tighten them (c-cl) and loosen them (cl). Got it? Don't forget and screw up your left pedal and crank!

4. All threaded parts are easy to strip (that means ruin the threads). Before putting any two together, make sure they are the same size and thread type; start screwing one into the other BY HAND, slowly. If they resist each other, don't force their relationship. Back off. Get parts that groove before you use tools on them. And use only small tools to tighten up small bolts and nuts. Tightening those 8- and 9-mm nuts takes deftness with the digits, not beef with the biceps. Save the beef for hill climbs.

5. Nine-tenths of the work you do to solve any bike problem goes into finding out just where the problem is. Even if you know what's wrong in a general way, don't start dismantling things until you know exactly

what is amiss. You, your bike, and this book must work as a team; look closely at your bike as you go through the DIAGNOSIS or PROBLEMS section of the chapter that applies to your problem. Don't work on the bike without looking at the book, and don't read through a whole chapter of the book without looking at your bike. That way no parts will feel left out at the end.

6. Dismantle as little as possible to do any repair. When you have to take something apart, do so slowly, laying the parts out in a neat row, in the order they came off. Work over a rag or a T-shirt or a flat piece of paper or even bark off a dead tree limb, and put the row of parts on that work surface, so you don't lose parts in the weeds. The more careful you are as you dismantle a unit, the less time it'll take to find the parts and put the thing back together.

7. Think twice before attacking rust-frozen parts, especially if you are out in the backcountry. Is there any way you can get home without undoing them? If so, try it. You're liable to break those rusty parts as you try to loosen them up, and chances are you won't have replacements with you.

8. There are lots of ball bearings on a bicycle. Sometimes they are in sealed, replaceable cartridges. But most spend their time racing around in happy circles between *cones* and *cups*. Either the cone or the cup of each bearing unit is usually threaded, so you can adjust how much room the balls have to play in. You don't want too much play; just enough to let the balls roll smoothly. To adjust any bearing set, first loosen (c-cl, usually) the locknut or lockring that holds the whole unit in place, then tighten (usually cl) the threaded part that's easiest to get at until you feel it squeeze the ball bearings. Then back it off (c-cl) a bit; usually less than a quarter turn is enough. Finally, re-tighten the locknut or ring (cl) so everything stays nicely adjusted. Spin the part on its bearings. It should coast smoothly and gradually to a stop. See if you can wiggle it from side to side on the bearings. If it is free to wiggle more than a hair's breadth, or if it is not free to roll smoothly, readjust the thing. Keep those bearings oiled or greased, adjusted, and out of the rain, and they'll give you years of happy, free-rolling service. If your bike gets covered with mud or gritty dust, you can wash it off, but don't aim power-ful blasts of water, especially water with detergent in it (like at a do-it-yourself carwash), at any of the bear-ings. You can ruin bearings by washing the lubricant out of them; even "sealed" bearings can be ruined in this way.

9. Cultivate a keen ear for those little complaining noises your bike makes when it has problems, like grindy bearings, kerchunking chain, a clunking shock fork, or a slight creak-squeaking of a crank that is coming loose. You don't have to talk to your bike when you ride it—just listen to it affectionately, and take care of its minor complaints before they become major problems miles away from home. And speak-ing of being nice to your bike, here's a tip that'll save you a heap of trouble:

Always lay your bike down on the LEFT side. If you lay a multispeed bike on its right side, you can bend, bash, and misalign its tender gear-changing parts. If a multispeed bike FALLS on its right side, the gears are almost sure to go out of adjustment.

10. Find a good bike shop in the area where you do most of your riding. Good shops are not necessarily the big flashy ones; they are the ones with people who *care*. Do as much of your bike shopping as you can at a shop that cares, and send friends to get their bikes there. The prices may be a bit higher, but the value is also higher in the long run.

11. If you need help out in the country, don't be afraid to ask for it. Use discretion with strangers if you are riding alone, but if you are in a group, don't be shy about asking folks if you can use their tools or make a phone call. You'll be amazed at how many friendly folks there are out there; all you have to do is show a little politeness and humility.

When and Where to Ride

Ride during the daytime, on trails or roads where bikes are allowed. Don't ride on high ridges in lightning storms, don't ride in desert gullies during downpours, keep off farms where the farmers tend to shower visitors with shotgun pellets, and don't ride in blizzards at night unless you are an insomniac survivalist. Oh, hell, you can ride wherever and whenever you want. But if you go on rides that don't make sense, don't expect this book to save you from your own foolishness.

Quick Maintenance Check

When you're itching to go on a ride, you don't want to spend much time fooling around with your bike. Just check the following three items and you'll cover about nine-tenths of the causes for trouble encountered on bike rides.

1. **Chain:** Make sure it is clean and lubricated. Check it for excessive stretching and kinks, too. (See page 173.)

2. **Tires:** Make sure they're pumped up to the correct pressure and make sure the tube isn't bulging out anywhere. (See page 106.)

3. **Brakes:** Make sure they'll stop you. When you squeeze the levers, they should only go about two-thirds of the way to the handlebars before the brakes are fully applied. Check for frayed cables and loose or cockeyed brake shoes. (See pages 38, 54.)

Those are the most important items. There are a few other things you can look into if you have been getting any hints of trouble on previous rides. If your gears have been slipping or making weird noises, check the cables and adjustment. (See page 188.) If your cranks have been squeaking, check the mounting bolts for looseness (page 154); if your wheels are loose, tighten the nuts or the quick-release lever (page 114), or adjust the bearings (page 116). Check your seat (page 137), handlebars (page 68), and headset (page 78) for looseness, too.

Tools and Other Stuff to Take

You can't take every tool and spare part you might need for every imaginable repair. Take the mini-kit below on short rides, and put together a maxi-kit for longer treks, bike tours, and your shop at home. No matter what size ride you're going on, WEAR A HELMET. If you protect and use the gray matter inside your helmet, it'll help you work out makeshift solutions to your bike problems with the tools you have at hand. And you'll find that gray matter, unlike most tools, improves with use under pressure.

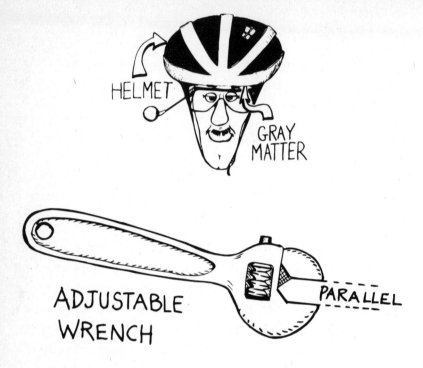

HELMET

GRAY MATTER

ADJUSTABLE WRENCH

PARALLEL

MINI-KIT

1. **Adjustable Wrench** (crescent wrench). Get a good one. Attributes of a good one are a forged body, milled and hardened jaws, and a precise adjusting action. To test a wrench, open the adjustable jaw a little and see if you can wiggle it in such a way that it moves up and down in relation to the body of the tool. A good adjustable wrench will wiggle very little, and the jaws will stay parallel. The six-inch size is best. Some people hacksaw the end of the handle off to make the thing even smaller.

2. **Screwdriver/Pocket Knife.** A screwdriver with a forged steel shank and a thin blade end is best. A pocket knife with a screwdriver blade will work fine for most adjusting screws, and it's good to have a knife for things like slicing cheese for lunch out in the open

country. Just don't do any heavy prying or tire-removing (see below) with your pocket knife or screwdriver blade. The screwdriver tip should be about ¼ inch wide and the shank 4 or 5 inches long.

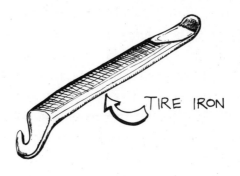

TIRE IRON

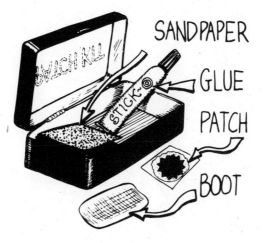

SANDPAPER

GLUE

PATCH

BOOT

3. **Tire Patch Kit and Tire Irons.** A patch kit can be bought as a unit from any bike shop. It should have a tube of glue (keep the cap on tight or the glue dries up), several small and large patches (the kind that taper out to thin, flexible edges are best), and something to scrape a rough spot on the tube, like a swatch of sandpaper.

You can buy patches that are self-sticking, too. They require no messy glue. They are not as durable as the glue-on type, but I've known some that lasted over a year. Add a boot to your patch kit; to make one, cut out a ¾-inch by 3-inch piece of thin sidewall from an old bike tire. A good boot can rescue a tire with a bad slit in it, or at least make the slit tire usable to get you home. Each tire iron should have a thin, smooth, rounded prying end, and a hook on the other end to fit onto a spoke after you have pried up on your tire bead. Make sure the tire irons are top quality, either steel or heavy-duty plastic; cheapo thick or sharp-edged ones make holes in your tube like a screwdriver if you aren't real adept at using them.

4. **Spare Tube.** It can be a real lightweight one; roll it up tight and it'll fit in the small pouch you use to carry your mini-kit.

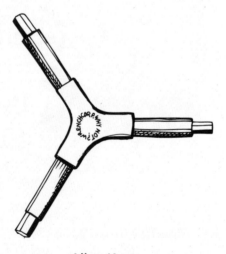

Allen Keys

5. **Allen Keys** (Allen wrenches). Depending on what kind of bike parts you have, you may need sizes ranging from 1.5 mm to 6 mm. You can get a "Y" tool with

4 mm, 5 mm, and 6 mm, which is fine if your bike requires only those sizes. Some bikes have parts that require other keys. For these bikes you might get a folding set of Allen keys that has 5 or more keys. Park Tool Company also makes a dogbone-shaped set that's great. If you get a new part that requires an odd size Allen key, buy the wrench at the same time you get the part, and add the wrench to your mini-kit. Keep them all together with a rubber band so you don't lose the little buggers.

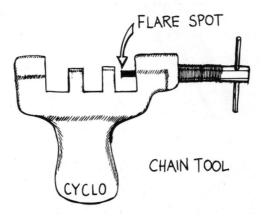

FLARE SPOT

CHAIN TOOL

CYCLO

6. **Chain Tool.** For driving rivets in and out of the chain. Get one that is the right size for your width of chain, either standard or narrow. Inexpensive ones work, but don't last long. Save the spare tip if you get one with yours; the tip tends to pop out of the tool and get lost. If you're plagued with tip loss, you can blow a bunch of money on a heavy-duty plier-type chain tool, or you can keep a close eye on the tip of your cheap chain tool; when you see it flaring out like the butt end of a wedge where it's been hammered, as shown in the Ritchey Tool illustration on page 22, carefully file that flare off with a small metal file, so the tip won't get stuck inside the chain's sideplates.

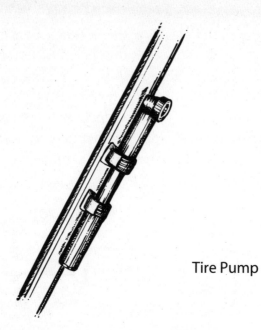

Tire Pump

7. **Tire Pump.** Get either a well-made bike frame pump or a strong mini-pump. It can be small, as long as it has a head that fits securely on your tire valves, and solid working parts that won't fail when you really need them. Many mountain bikers carry mini-pumps in their fanny packs; they run no risk of having the pump getting joggled off their bike frame, and they run no risk of having the pump stolen if they leave the bike unattended. But it takes a lot of pumping to inflate a tire with a mini-pump. If you get lots of flats and need a full-size frame pump, strap it to the frame with a velcro-binding pump strap so it can't get joggled off.

8. **Friend.** No description needed. Take a good one on all long rides, though, for parts-holding, morale-boosting, and, if things get really bad, help-fetching.

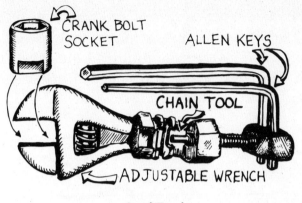

Cool Tool

9. **A quarter and a couple of dollars.** Not as important as a friend, especially when you are far from "civilization," but handy for calling home from the nearest gas station, or buying emergency food from country stores.

You can put all the tools in the mini-kit inside a small cloth pouch, such as an under-the-saddle pack, and strap this pouch to the rails under the back of your seat. There are even multi-tools, such as the Cool Tool, Ritchey Tool, or the Topeak Alien, that combine things like a wrench, chain tool, Allen keys, headset wrench, and other tools, so you can save weight and bulk in your mini-kit. The Cool Tool, Ritchey Tool, and Topeak Alien work well for many jobs if you use them carefully. Some other multi-tools are almost worthless, they are so poorly designed. Shop carefully if you get a multi-tool.

MAXI-KIT
for long treks or your home shop

10. **Cable Cutters.** The best ones are the heavy-duty bicycle cable clippers that grab the cable in a diamond-shaped hole and shear it off clean. Park Tool Company makes great cable cutters. Expensive, but

worth it. The chomping types of wire cutters (such as those on needlenose pliers and diagonal cutters) will do, but if they are dull or flimsy, they mash the ends of the cables; you have to thread the cables through their housings *before* you cut them to size, and re-threading is a real pain.

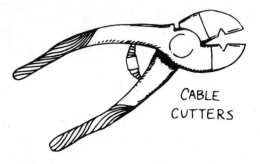

CABLE
CUTTERS

11. Pliers. The hardware-store variety are OK. Channel-lock pliers are better. Some jobs require vise-grip pliers. To be used only as directed. NOT a valid replacement for a good crescent wrench.

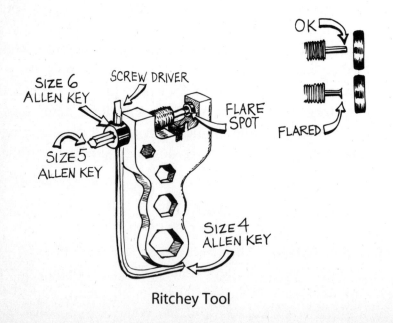

Ritchey Tool

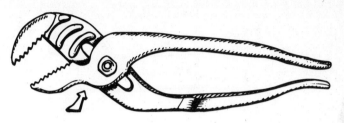

CHANNEL LOCK

12. **Lubricants.** Keep light oil such as ATF (automatic transmission fluid) or a bike lubricant such as Triflow or Finish Line Dry Lube for your chain and other moving parts. You can get tiny little containers of some lubricants, perfect for stuffing in your tool bag or mini-kit. In a pinch, you can use motor oil, chainsaw oil, or even salad oil (I'll never forget the hot dusty day when I stopped at the mountain cabin of my friend Anne Scott, and she gave me some olive oil for my dried-up chain; thanks, Anne!) to lubricate your chain. The only lubes I steer clear of are ones like liquid wrench and WD-40; they contain penetrating chemicals that soon dry up. Use fine cycle grease for all bearings.

13. **Hub Spanners.** Buy a set of two that fit your hubs, either a 13-14 mm set, or a 15-16 mm set. Campagnolo and Park make good ones. They cost a lot, but they are essential to wheel bearing adjustment. Trek makes "Wrench Force" ones that are cheaper and at least as durable.

14. **Pedal Spanner.** Looks like an oversize hub spanner. Should have a 15-mm end and a $\frac{9}{16}$-inch end, to fit different makes of pedals. Get a forged, high-quality

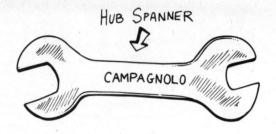

one, like the Trek "Wrench Force" one, so it won't wear out.

15. **Spoke Wrench.** A cheap little tool that can get you into a lot of expensive trouble. That's why they're so cheap, and available at any bike shop that will take on a wheel you ruin. So use ONLY as directed.

16. **Y Socket Tool.** A nifty little thing that fits easily in your hand, fits all of the 8-, 9-, and 10-mm bolts and nuts on bikes, and gives you enough leverage to tighten them, but not strip them, if you take it easy. You can also get a Y Allen key tool, as described in the MINI-KIT section above.

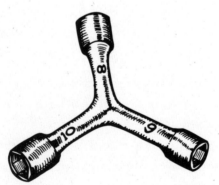

17. **Headset Spanner.** If you have a road bike or a cruiser, consider getting a wrench that fits the top locknut and the threaded race on your headset. This wrench,

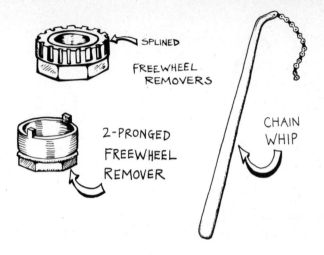

SPLINED

FREEWHEEL
REMOVERS

2-PRONGED
FREEWHEEL
REMOVER

CHAIN
WHIP

called a headset spanner, looks somewhat like a hub spanner, but is much larger. If you have a threadless headset, as most mountain bikes and hybrid bikes do, you won't need this tool.

18. **Chain Whip and/or Freewheel Remover.** A chain whip is a short length of bike chain with a handle attached. A freewheel remover is a big nut with either splines or two prongs on it, depending on what kind of free-wheel it fits. You only need these tools for changing the gear cogs or sprockets on your rear wheel. Unless you ride lots and ride hard, you won't have to do this job more than once or twice a decade, so you might want to skip this tool and let a shop take care of free-wheel switches. Older bikes have freewheels that require a remover. Newer bikes have cassettes for the cogs, which require use of a narrow freewheel remover to unscrew a lockring on the cassette and a chain whip to hold the cogs still while you unscrew that lockring.

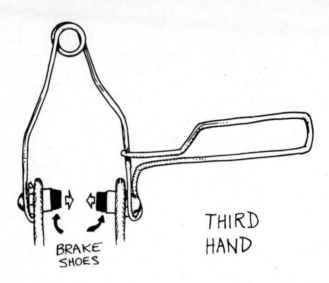

THIRD
HAND

BRAKE
SHOES

19. **Third Hand.** A springy, curvy little wire thing made for holding brake shoes against the wheel. Bike shops have them.

20. **Crank remover tool.** Rarely needed; consists of a threaded outer part that screws into the hole for your crank mounting bolt, and a threaded post in the middle that pushes against the end of your axle to pull the crank off of it. Get one that fits your cranks if you work on your bike lots and don't want to depend on a shop or bike mechanic friend for one.

21. **Spare Parts.** Spokes (exactly the same sizes as the ones on your wheels, of course), brake and gear cables, a few links of chain (like the extra links you get when you replace your chain), and maybe an elastic "bungee" cord or two.

FOUND AND BORROWED TOOLS

You'd be amazed at the things you can use for tools if you're stuck out in the middle of nowhere. A rock becomes a

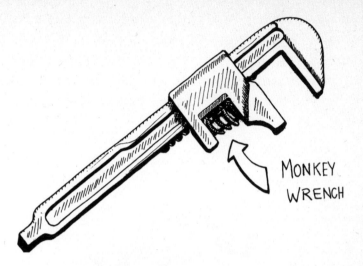

MONKEY
WRENCH

hammer or an anvil. A stick becomes a lever. A tree limb becomes a bike stand. Hey, we humans got along fine with
such tools for millions of years. And then there are the tools
that you can borrow from a friendly farmer or woods-
person. I've met many farmers who chased me off their land
for trespassing, but I've never met a country mechanic who
wouldn't let me use a wrench or a pair of channel lock pliers if I asked politely. In fact, I have more trouble trying to
politely tell backwoods mechanics that I'd rather fix the
bike myself, rather than turning it over to them. I'll never
forget the guy who wanted to take his welding torch to my
bent Cinelli forks.

WHERE TO GET TOOLS AND PARTS

I recommend you get all parts and tools from the shop
where you got your bike. Then you'll be sure to get stuff
that fits, and you'll be giving the shop valued business. If
you don't live within 50 miles of a shop, you can get a catalog for tools and parts; see the latest issue of a bike magazine, such as *Bicycling Magazine*, for catalog ads. Whatever
you do, though, don't go into a shop and use up lots of their
time and energy finding out what part or tool fits your bike,
and then leave the shop and go order the part or tool from

a catalog. That may save you a little money, but it will cost you a lot of respect from the bike shop. Next time you have a pretzled wheel, they may not be willing to straighten it. And catalogs can't straighten wheels. Nor can they affect whether you are respected or not by the local cycling community.

Penny-Farthing with One-Shoe Brake

CHAPTER 2

Brakes

OVERALL BRAKE SYSTEM DIAGNOSIS: Your bike has either hand brakes or a foot (coaster) brake. The coaster brake only stops the rear wheel, and is not as efficient as good hand brakes, but it will work for children and for low-speed cruiser cycling for adults. You might have a special hand-actuated hub or disk brake, but these gizmos are too specialized for me to cover.

Scuffy Skillman One-Foot Brake

C If you have a foot or coaster brake (the kind you pedal backward to apply), and the thing sticks, or it doesn't slow you down very well, or it slips, you have to take the rear wheel off the bike and take the hub apart to fix the brake. This takes time and patience. But the problem is usually relatively simple, so if you're short on cash and long on time and patience, carefully follow the Overhaul procedure on page 52 and you'll probably have the brake working fine in a day or so.

M R If you are having problems with hand brakes, you may have to look at the whole brake system to find out just what is causing the problem. The following paragraphs describe the two basic problems you can have with brakes; read them to find out which part of the brake system you have to work on to solve your problem.

M R *Brakes don't go on.* The problem is probably a loose or broken cable, or an entire brake system that is so rusty or mud-clogged that the parts are locked together. Inspect the brake cable for breaks or frayed places. (See Cable PROBLEMS for more info.) If the whole system for either your front or your back brake is rusty or clogged, try cleaning it with a rag or your shirttail, apply some lubricant if you have any along, and work the mechanism by hand while squeezing the hand lever; if that doesn't get it working, ride home slowly using your other brake, then replace the cable and overhaul the mechanism if necessary, as described later in this chapter.

M R *Brakes don't go off.* Something is stuck somewhere in your brake system so one or both of the brake shoes won't let go of the wheel rim when you let go of the brake handle. Any of the three units of the brake system—the Hand Lever, the Cable, or the Mechanism—could be hung up. If your brakes get the "stickies" (a malady about as common to brakes as the common cold is to us), first find out which unit is stuck. Apply the brake. Move the hand lever back to its released position. If it moves freely, it's OK and you know the snag is in the cable and/or the mechanism. If the hand lever doesn't move freely, it has the stickies. (See Hand Lever PROBLEMS.)

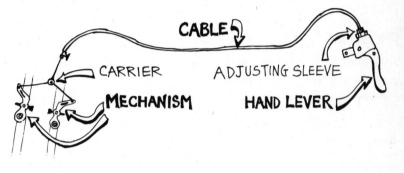

2-1 The Three Units of a Brake System

M R If the trouble is in the cable or mechanism, pull the little transverse cable end out of its notch on one of the cantilevers (on road bikes, release the quick-release lever on the brake mechanism) so the brakes become loose. Then tug a little on the carrier with one hand and operate the brake hand lever with the other hand. When you release the lever, does the cable fail to slip back towards your tugging hand? If so, and the lever is OK, then you can bet the cable has the stickies. (See Cable PROBLEMS.)

M R Cable OK? That leaves the brake mechanism. Try reaching through the spokes of the wheel with your fingers and squeezing and releasing the brake shoes. If one or both don't spring away from the rim when you let go of them, or if one shoe is cockeyed, see Mechanism PROBLEMS.

M R If you have problems other than the two above, see the unit that has a problem. For example, if you can't reach the lever because your fingers are too short, see the *Hand Lever* section, below.

Hand Lever

DESCRIPTION: Ⓜ Ⓡ The thing you grab to put on hand brakes. The unit is attached to the bars either by one or two easy-to-get-at mounting bolts on the side of the post, or by one hard-to-get-at mounting bolt down inside the post. (See Illustrations 2-2, 2-3, 2-4.)

PROBLEMS: Ⓜ Ⓡ *Stickies.* If you have taken a spill, the problem is usually a bent lever, or dirt and rust stuck in the part of the lever where it pivots. See if the lever is twisted out of line. Compare it with the other one. If the lever is bent, try to straighten it with your bare hands, holding the part that mounts to the handlebar in one hand and bending the lever with the other. It may help to stick a screwdriver between the lever and the post or housing (on road bike units), but go easy with the screwdriver. Just straighten the lever unit enough to get you home. Get some oil if you can and squirt a bit onto the hand lever axle or pivot. If the lever seems weak or still partially sticky, make sure you replace the whole unit before your next ride. (See *Hand lever broken*, below.) You don't want that brake to break the next time you really need it.

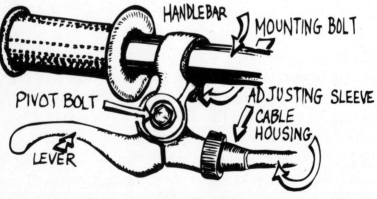

2-2 Mountain Bike Brake Lever

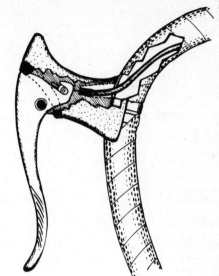

2-3 Aero Brake Lever

HAND LEVER

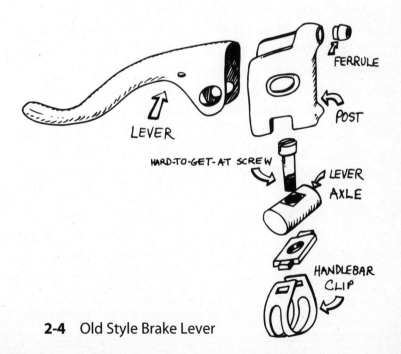

FERRULE

LEVER

POST

HARD-TO-GET-AT SCREW

LEVER
AXLE

HANDLEBAR
CLIP

2-4 Old Style Brake Lever

Ⓜ If the pivot is dirty or rusty and has tightened up, loosen (c-cl) the pivot bolt about two turns. Then squeeze on the lever and release it a bunch of times to work out any dirt in there. If you have some lubricant with you, squirt a dab in there. Then tighten (cl) the bolt. If the lever action gets stiff, back off (c-cl) the pivot bolt a quarter turn or so. Most pivot bolts have self-locking nuts, so they don't come loose if you don't tighten them up all the way. Even if the pivot bolt is loose after you back it off a bit, it will probably stay in there until you get home. Just make sure you take the brake lever apart when you get there; all you have to do is loosen (c-cl) the pivot bolt all the way, take the lever out, then clean it and replace any bent or munched parts, and reassemble it.

Ⓜ Ⓡ If the ***whole hand lever is loose,*** so it slips around on the handlebars, you have to tighten (cl) the mounting bolt that holds it to the bars. On most mountain bike brake hand levers, you need an Allen key to do the tightening. If the hand lever slips out of place while it is loose, get it lined up parallel to the other one (so it points neither too high nor too low), then tighten (cl) the mounting bolt firmly.

Ⓡ On road bike brake levers, the screw that tightens the lever clamp on the handlebar is often down inside the lever post. To get at it, you may have to release the brake cable (that means take the tension out of the cable so that the brake lever relaxes and swings freely). Whatever kind of brake you want to release, you have to grab the brake mechanism and squeeze the brake shoes against the rim. Use the third hand tool if you have one. Stick it through the spokes of the wheel and stretch the wire loops over the brake-shoe nuts. On most road bikes, there will be some kind of quick-release gizmo. It will be at or just above the brake mechanism. (See Illustration 2-10.) It is usually a little lever that you can pull toward the side of the mechanism, to partially release the brake.

▣ Take the resulting looseness in the cable back up to the hand lever and you're ready to get at the post-tightening screw. If you don't have a quick-release lever, loosen (c-cl) the cable anchor bolt that holds the end of the cable at the brake mechanism. (See Illustrations 2-8 and 2-10.) Try to avoid pulling the end of the cable all the way out of the cable anchor bolt, especially if the end of the cable is frayed into strands. A frayed cable end is hard to get back through the little hole in the cable anchor bolt.

▣ When you have loosened the brake cable by hook or by crook, pull the brake lever all the way down, as if you are jamming the brake on. Look down inside the hand lever post. Aha! That little Allen screw head or hex nut down there is what you have been trying to get at. If you have the type with an allen screw head, you're in luck. Just wiggle an Allen wrench down in there and tighten up the screw, clockwise. Counterclockwise loosens the thing, but don't loosen it until it comes out. Getting it back in is a tricky operation.

▣ If your model has a hexbolt head down there, you need a socket to tighten that bolt. It might be an 8-mm bolt head if the bike is old or fancy. Otherwise, it is probably a 9-mm nut. Use the proper socket on a Y wrench (see page 24) or use a standard socket tool to tighten (cl) the bolt down in there. Don't try to use a tool that won't work, like your fingers, or a crescent wrench, or a vise-grip, or your teeth.

▣ When you have tightened the mounting screw or nut, you have to reset the brake by reversing whichever procedure you used to loosen the cable. A third hand is a big help. If you run into trouble, see **Brakes loose** in the *Brake Cables* section.

 If you ***can't reach the hand lever*** because your fingers are too short or the lever sticks out too far, first loosen the brakes a little (see ***Adjusting the brakes,*** below), then look on or under the main body of the hand lever unit and see if there is a small screw or Allen bolt that doesn't have an obvious purpose. Turn the screw or bolt (if your brakes have one), and you should see the hand lever move closer or farther from the handlebars. Fiddle with the thing until the lever is just close enough for you to reach and *no closer.* Re-adjust the brakes if they are too tight now. Beware: If you have to adjust the lever so it is more than one-third of the way in toward the bar, you are probably limiting your rim clearance and braking range too much. Consider getting special short-reach levers from a custom-bike dealer.

  Hand lever broken or badly munched. You need to replace it. You really smacked that tree with the bars, didn't you? Hope your knuckles are better off than your brake lever.

  To replace the hand lever, first you have to loosen the cable and slip the barrel end out of the handle.

 To loosen a mountain bike brake cable, you go to the mechanism end and pull the removable end of the short transverse cable out of its slot in one of the cantilevers. This gives you a little slack in the whole system. Then, back at the hand lever, twiddle and twist the adjusting barrel and locknut to line up the slots in them, then slip the barrel end out of the hand lever.

 To loosen a road bike brake cable, just loosen (c-cl) the anchor bolt on the mechanism. Then you can pull the whole cable backwards out of the housing, until the mechanism end comes out of the hand lever. Then go on to the replacement procedure, down a few paragraphs.

 Once the cable is out of the way, you have to remove the bar ends and handlebar grip. On most bar ends, you just loosen a binder bolt with an Allen key, and the thing slides right off. Handlebar grips can be tougher to remove. Try twisting and pulling slowly first. No go? You have to get serious. If the grip covers the end of the bar (i.e., you have no bar ends), you can poke a hole in that end cover (if there isn't a hole there already) and blow compressed air in there as you twist and pull the grip off. If you're a bagpipe player, you may have enough lung power to exert the necessary air pressure; otherwise, go to a bike or car shop that has an air compressor, put the cleaning nozzle on the end of their hose, stick the nozzle into your hole in the grip-end, then blast air in there while you twist and pull on the grip. Still no luck? Some grips are glued on. You have to cut them off with a razor knife, then get a replacement grip.

Ⓜ If you have a grip-shift gear changer, loosen (c-cl) the Allen bolt that cinches the unit onto the handlebar and slide the whole shifter off the bar.

Ⓜ OK, so you've got your bar end and hand grip or grip-shift unit off your handlebar. Now all you have to do to remove the hand lever is loosen (c-cl) the mounting bolt, then slide the lever unit off the bar. Get an exact replacement, if possible; it feels weird to use two different types of brake levers.

Ⓜ Slide the new lever unit on, twist it on the bar to line it up parallel with the other lever (so the new one points neither up nor down too much), then tighten (cl) the mounting bolt.

Ⓜ Slip on your hand grip. If you ride in lots of mud, use rubber cement as a combo lube/glue: when it's wet, the grip slides on easy; when it dries, the grip stays put, no matter how wet and gooey your hands get. Just remember that you'll have to cut the grip off if you ever need to remove it.

Ⓜ Put your bar end on again, twist it to line it up with its mate, and tighten (cl) the binder bolt. Then put the cable back in the way it came out, lining up the slots as you go.

Do a little ***adjusting the brakes***, as in the *Brake Cable* section in this chapter, and you'll be set to go again (and STOP, too!).

Replacing the brake lever on a road bike requires that you loosen (c-cl) the mounting bolt. See the ***whole hand lever loose*** section, above, for how to loosen the cable and get access to the bolt. After you loosen (c-cl) it, take the handlebar tape off the end of the bar, then slide off the bent hand lever unit and slide on a new one. Tighten the mounting bolt inside that hand lever unit. Then re-tighten the brake cable, re-tape the end of the bar, and you're set to go.

Brake Cables

DESCRIPTION: Ⓜ Ⓡ The brake cable runs from a notch or hole in the hand lever, through an end ferrule or an adjustable sleeve, which fits or screws into the brake lever post, then through a cable housing (which is sometimes interrupted so that the cable runs bare next to a frame tube), another end ferrule, and finally, through a carrier and/or an anchor bolt that holds the cable at its mechanism end. (See Illustrations 2-1, 2-5, 2-8, and 2-10.)

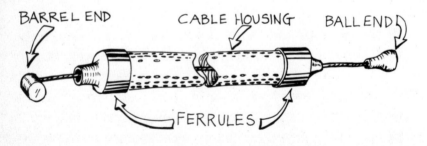

BARREL END   CABLE HOUSING   BALL END

FERRULES

2-5 Brake Cable and Ends

PROBLEMS: Ⓜ Ⓡ *Brakes loose.* Imagine this: You are screaming down Kamikaze at Mammoth and you come flying around a blind curve just a wee bit too fast, and suddenly you find yourself heading for a bathtub-size boulder. You slam on the brakes. Nothing happens for a terribly long instant. The next thing you realize is that the ground is coming up at you.

Agh. To avoid this type of nightmare, keep your brakes adjusted.

Ⓜ Ⓡ *Adjusting the brakes* usually means tightening the cable. How tight is tight enough? Most shops do brakes so you only have to squeeze the lever about halfway to the handlebars to apply them fully. Some people (and I'm one of them) like their brakes a bit looser than this, so the lever goes most of the way to the handlebar before the brakes are fully applied. This makes sense, because it lets you grip the bars with most of your fingers while applying the brakes with just two slightly extended fingers. Short, "two-finger" brake hand levers are good for the same reason, as long as they give you enough leverage. But no matter what your brake setup, you should never let either brake get so loose that the handle goes all the way to the handlebar without stopping the wheel.

Ⓜ Ⓡ *Minor adjustment* will usually be enough to get you home. See if there is an adjusting sleeve on your brake handle. On most road bikes the adjusting sleeve is at the mechanism end of the cable. You can adjust these sleeves by hand, unless they are mud-clogged or rusted tight. Loosen (c-cl) the lockring and then turn the sleeve counterclockwise too, even though this may not seem right to you at first. It tightens the cable, because it has the effect of making the cable housing longer, which tightens up the brakes. After adjusting the sleeve, try out the brake. If it works OK now, tighten (cl) the lockring hard against the hand lever or brake mechanism (not against the adjusting sleeve) and you're ready to go. If it's hard to tighten up the cable, try squeezing the brake shoes in against the rim with one hand while you use the other hand to fiddle with the adjusting sleeve; taking the tension off the cable often makes it easier to tighten the brakes. If you cannot get the cable tight enough even by turning the adjusting sleeve all the way out (c-cl), you have to do a major adjustment with the cable anchor bolt. Turn the sleeve back in (cl) until it is at least halfway to its loosest setting, then tighten (cl) the lockring against the hand lever or mechanism and go on to the next paragraph.

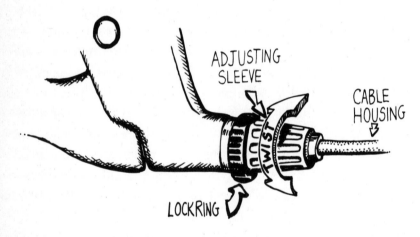

2-6   Adjusting Sleeve

Ⓜ Ⓡ A ***major brake adjustment*** is hard to do on the trail or road if you don't have two wrenches, or at least a wrench and a good pair of pliers, along with a friend who's willing to lend a strong hand or two so you can loosen and tighten the cable anchor bolt. Look at Illustrations 2-8 and 2-10 to see where the anchor bolt is on your brake mechanism. Most mechanisms have the anchor bolt on one end of a cantilever or brake arm. On many mountain bikes, there is also a secondary anchor bolt that pinches the cable at the carrier, as in Illustration 2-8.

M R Before tightening the cable, see if you can loosen the brake. On mountain bikes, undo one end of the short transverse cable from its socket in the cantilever. On road bikes, pull the release lever on the mechanism down, so it loosens the cable.

M R Then get a wrench or the pliers fitted tight on the head of the anchor bolt. If you have a friend to hold the wrench or pliers on there good and tight, it makes the job a lot easier. While the anchor bolt is held still, loosen (c-cl) the nut until the cable can slide through the anchor bolt. Then move the anchor bolt up the cable about a quarter of an inch (the anchor bolt is about a quarter-inch thick, to give you an idea). You can gauge how far you are moving it by looking at the squished-flat section of the cable where the anchor bolt used to be. When you have moved the anchor bolt up (that is, you have pulled the cable through the bolt), tighten (cl) the nut on the anchor bolt firmly, until you can see that it has actually flattened out the cable in the little hole. You should use both tools yourself to do the last hard tightening of the anchor bolt and nut (not *too* hard, though, or you will strip the threads). Un-release the brake (mountain bikers, hook up the short transverse cable; road-ies, push the release lever up so it's tight) and test the brake. If it's a bit too tight or loose, adjust it with the sleeve at the hand lever end of the cable as described in the **minor adjustment,** above. Brake still way too loose? Do the major adjustment over.

M If your brake has a secondary anchor bolt in the carrier, you may need to adjust it a bit one way or the other so the mechanism is balanced, with both brake shoes the same distance from the walls of the rim, as shown in Illustration 2-8. To adjust the secondary anchor bolt, loosen (c-cl) it, then slide the carrier up and down on the main brake cable until the brake pads are equidistant from the wheel rim. Then tighten (cl) the secondary anchor bolt.

M R If a **_cable is broken,_** and you're out on the trail or road, the best thing to do is make sure the other brake is adjusted well enough to work, then ride home with extreme caution and replace the broken cable with a new one.

M R You can **_replace the cable_** if you brought along a spare cable with you on a ride, or if you are at home. First undo the anchor bolt on the broken cable and undo the secondary anchor bolt in the carrier if you have one, then pull the end of the cable out of the anchor bolt(s). Next, pull the cable out of the housing and ferrules, all the way back up to the handle. At the hand lever, loosen (c-cl) the lockring for the adjusting sleeve, if there is one, then twiddle with the lockring and the sleeve until the slots are lined up so you can swing the cable down and out. The barrel end will still be held in the lever itself; line up the cable with the release slot in the lever, then push the barrel sideways to get it out. On road bikes, you have to push and wiggle the ball end out of its socket in the lever.

M R Grease the new cable and thread it in carefully; slide the barrel end into the hole in the lever sideways, then slip the cable into the slots in the lever, the adjusting sleeve, and the lockring, keeping them all lined up as you go. Push the cable through the housing and ferrules, thread it through the secondary anchor bolt in the carrier if you have one, then through the anchor bolt. Tighten your new cable up as described in the **_major brake adjustment_** procedure earlier in this section.

R If you have an old-fashioned type of hand lever with no nifty slots to slide the cable out, removal is trickier. You may be able to jiggle the barrel end around until it pops out of its holder in the lever, or you may have to cut off the frayed and broken end of the cable, then push the whole thing backwards through the housing and the lever and out to freedom.

M R If *both* cables are broken and you are miles from home, you have to figure out some way to use the rear cable on your front brake. First look at the broken end of the rear cable. Is the break near the mechanism end? If so, and if the break is a pretty clean one, all you have to do is take the cables out of their housings and put the rear one in the front brake system, using the ***replace the cable*** procedure, above. Make sure you get the little ball or barrel at the end of the cable set firmly in its notch in the hand lever, then thread the cable through the little ferrules and the housing on down to the front brake mechanism. If the cable end is too frayed to go through the housing, you have to find your way to a farmer or somebody who has a pair of good wire cutters to clip off the frayed end. When you have a good clean cut on the end of the cable, thread it in.

M R Tighten your makeshift front brake, as in the ***major brake adjustment*** procedure earlier in this section. If you have extra cable left over, wind it up in a little coil and tie the coil with the end so it'll stay out of the works as you ride cautiously home. Mountain bikers: Undo the rear brake's transverse cable, too, so it won't flop down and catch a knobby. Do a complete replacement of both your brake cables when you get home, as described above.

M R ***Cable sticky.*** If you've ascertained, by the diagnostic method in the OVERALL BRAKE SYSTEM DIAGNOSIS section for the brakes, that your cable is sticking, it's probably because the thing is either rusty, mud-clogged, or kinked.

M If the cable is rusty or mud-clogged, you can grab the carrier with one hand and the hand lever with the other and just horse the thing back and forth a whole bunch of times; with luck, you'll loosen up enough of the crud inside the cable housing and ferrules so that the cable can do its job. If you have some lubricant, apply it at the places where the cable disappears into the housing and work it in as you horse the cable back and forth.

■ ■ If you are at home, or if you are out on the trail or road and have some time and lubricant, release the tension on the cable. Mountain bikers, pull the removable end of the transverse cable out of its slot in the cantilever. On a road bike, use the quick-release lever on the brake mechanism to loosen the brakes. Then pull the hand lever all the way to the bars; put oil or grease on the shiny (or rusty) sections of the cable that you have just pulled out of the housings. These normally unseen sections of the cable are usually the parts that cause the stickies. If they are really rusty, you need to replace the cable.

■ ■ If the cable housing has a kink (a sharp, unnatural bend in the springy, plastic-covered tube that the cable runs through), all you have to do is get a firm bare-handed grip on the housing on either side of that kink and straighten it. If the kink is at one end of the housing, like right next to the hand lever, make a mental note to loosen and remove the cable when you get home, then snip off the bent end of the housing, thread the cable back in, and reset the brakes. Don't try this out in the backcountry unless you have a good pair of cable clippers along. You may not be able to get the brake back together if the end of the cable is frayed. If this is the case, just straighten the kink as well as you can with your bare hands and ride home to your cable-cutting tool.

■ ■ If you are at home and have a good cable-cutting tool, take the cable out of the kinked housing, then either cut the kinked end off the housing, or replace the whole length of housing. Either way, you'll need to cut the housing; this takes a little know-how.

■ ■ To make a clean housing cut, one that doesn't have a burr digging into the brake cable, either snip it crisply with

RIGHT   WRONG (BURR)

2-7   Clean Cut and Burr in Housing End

your diamond-hole cable clipper (this works best if you have braided housing), or use diagonal clippers and slowly squeeze in on the cable housing. Wiggle and twist as you squeeze, so that the blades go in between the coils of the housing wire, instead of mashing a coil flat. When the clipper has worked its way slowly into a slot between the coils, squeeze harder and twist the clipper as you cut through. Twist the clippers sort of like you're popping the cap off a soda bottle with a bottle opener, only sideways. Check the new end of the cable housing for burrs. (See Illustration 2-7.) Is there one pointing out into the air? You can clip it off with the mashing type clippers, or file it down. If there's a burr sticking into the hole in the middle of the housing, you have to make another cut. Remember to twist as you cut. It takes a little practice. But don't use a housing with a burr that's going to dig into your cable and gradually ruin it. Ever notice how you only break a shoelace when you're in a hurry? The same logic works with brake cables. When a brake cable snaps, it's usually when you really need it.

Brake Mechanism

DESCRIPTION: There are different kinds of brake mechanisms on the different kinds of bikes. Each paragraph below covers the mechanism for the type of bike in the paragraph flag at the beginning. If you have a hybrid bike, the brakes are probably like those on mountain bikes.

Ⓜ Most mountain and hybrid mountain/city bikes have cantilever brakes. They have two pivots, one on each side of the wheel. The pivot bolts screw into mounts, which are usually brazed to the seat stays of the bike frame. This means they are very simple, light, and strong, but if you bend or smash the pivot and mount, it takes major surgery to replace it.

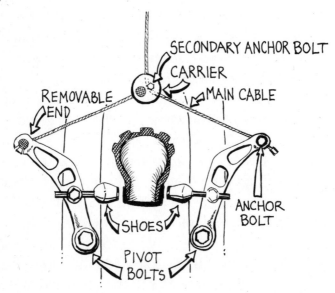

2-8 Cantilever Brake

Ⓜ Many newer mountain bikes have V-brake mechanisms. These are really just cantilever brakes with the cantilevers pointing straight up and a single cable pulling the arms together, instead of a main cable and a transverse cable. They are very simple and reliable mechanisms, even lighter than standard cantilevers, in some cases. Kudos to Ben Capron and others, for bringing us this brake from the arcane world of antique motorcycles. One word of caution about V-brakes: use them gently. They work. You put them on, and the wheel tends to stop, RIGHT NOW. Also, most V-brake models require that the brake shoes sit very close to the wheel rim, even when the brake is fully released. So you have to keep the brakes adjusted carefully, and you have to keep your wheels straight so the rims don't rub against those nearby brake shoes. If you have V-brakes on your bike, use the instructions in this chapter for cantilever brakes to do any adjustments and repairs. The only differences will be in the steps that deal with the cable, and dealing with the cable and anchor bolt on a V-brake is so simple it requires no additional explanation.

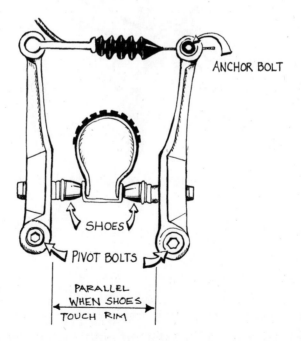

2-9 V-Brakes

R Most road bikes have side-pull brake mechanisms, or caliper brakes. The two arms, or calipers, pivot around one pivot bolt, and the brake cable pulls the arms together from one side. Some have two pivots, one for each caliper. These caliper mechanisms are time-tested, and if they are well-made, they can be light and strong. They don't deliver quite as much braking power as similar-quality cantilever brakes, but for road riding, if they are used carefully (that means using both brakes, and using the front ones a bit more than the rear ones as you stop), they work just fine.

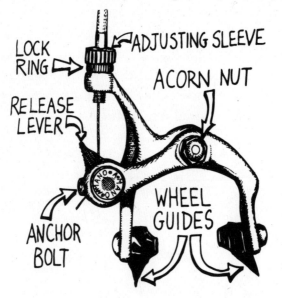

2-10   Side-pull or Caliper Brake

C Cruiser bikes and most children's bikes, except the racey BMX models, have coaster or foot-powered brakes, with a mechanism inside the rear hub. They are usually trouble-free, but they can wear out. If you have problems with a coaster brake, try working a little oil into the hub from the sides, and if that doesn't help, do the overhaul procedure on page 58.

PROBLEMS: Ⓜ Ⓡ *One-shoe drag.* One of the brake shoes refuses to come off the rim of your wheel when you release the brakes. First check to make sure the wheel isn't loose and/or cockeyed. Push the wheel all the way into its drop-out (fork-end slot) in the frame and tighten the quick-release or axle nuts firmly. (See page 115 for details.)

Ⓜ Check the brake mechanism. If the carrier is the kind that the main cable passes through, as shown in Illustration 2-8, loosen the secondary anchor bolt in the carrier, adjust the position of the carrier so the brakes center, then retighten the secondary anchor bolt.

Ⓜ If the springs on the two sides of the brake are out of balance, on a cantilever or V-brake mechanism, fiddling with the transverse cable won't solve the one-shoe drag; you have to adjust the springs. On most cantilever and V-brakes, there is a wee Allen bolt or Phillips screw that you can adjust to center the brakes. On some cantilever units, such as the Dia Compe 986 set, there is a pivot bolt that you can put an Allen key into, and a thin adjusting nut between the body of the cantilever and the bike frame. Fit a hub spanner or the thin jaws of a Cool Tool on this adjusting nut. Loosen (c-cl) the pivot bolt with your Allen key, then reset the position of the adjusting nut so the brakes are centered. Hold the nut in that position while you tighten (cl) the pivot bolt with the Allen key.

Ⓜ On a few cantilever and V-brake models, you have to reset the spring on the cantilever of the dragging shoe. To do this, pull the removable end of the transverse cable out of its slot in one cantilever to loosen the brake, then loosen (c-cl) the pivot bolt for the dragging shoe cantilever about five to seven turns. Then grasp the whole cantilever unit and slip it out on the pivot bolt, until the end of the spring comes out of its little hole in the brake-mount plate. Then turn the cantilever so the spring end moves *up* to the next *higher* hole in the mount plate (there are usually three little holes, and you can often hook the spring in a notch at the top of the plate for one more extra-tight setting). Setting the spring tension this way is a pain; if you have a lot of trouble keeping your brake shoes centered, I recommend you switch to ones that are easy to adjust, like those with wee Allen bolts or Phillips screws.

🆁 Check to see whether the whole brake mechanism is loose on its pivot bolt. If it's loose, so that the whole thing waggles back and forth, and the tightening nut (see Illustration 2-11) turns freely, just tighten that nut up (cl) while holding the mechanism by the arms so that the rim is centered between the shoes. If the tightening nut isn't loose, see if there are flats on the fixed seating pad, as shown in Illustration 2-11. Slip a cone wrench (14-mm size, in most cases) onto those flats and twist the mechanism gently until the rim is centered between the shoes.

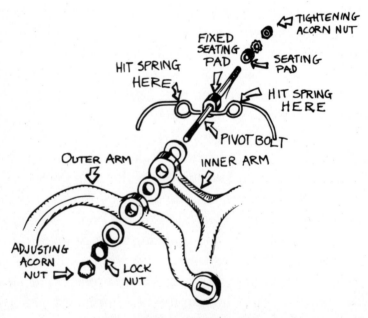

2-11 Side-pull Mechanism

◪ No handy flats on the seating pad? Try loosening (c-cl) the tightening acorn nut, then moving the mechanism by the arms to the right position, and tightening (cl) the nut again, making sure to hold the arms in the right position as you tighten the nut. If you have 2-pivot caliper brakes, you should be able to fix the one-shoe drag this way.

◪ Do you have single pivot calipers, and one brake shoe still insists on dragging along the rim? Take a good look at the shape of the fixed seating pad, which is against the frame tube on the mechanism side. (See Illustration 2-11.) It might be curved so it fits the surface of the frame. If so, the brake arms are going to come back to the same incorrect position no matter how many times you loosen the tightening nut.

◪ If all the above attempts fail, you have to bend the spring to move the pushed-in shoe off the rim. First tighten up (cl) the tightening nut. Take your hammer, your big screwdriver, and your knowledge of these tools' destructive tendencies, and approach the brake spring from above. (See Illustration 2-11.) Set the tip of your big screwdriver on the topmost point in the curve or loop of the brake spring on the side *where the shoe is off the rim*. Got that? The opposite side from where the shoe is rubbing. Set the screwdriver as near as possible to vertical (the handlebars or the seat may make it a little awkward; the longer the screwdriver, the better) and give the screwdriver handle a tap with the hammer, lightly. No luck? Shoe still on the rim? Be firmer. But go easy. It's all too easy to bend the spring too far, or put a big nick in it, or the frame tube, or your hand. Apply and release the brakes to check your shoe position when you think it's right. If one shoe or the other always seems to be dragging, maybe the spring is old and weak. It's time to overhaul the brake mechanism, as described below.

Ⓜ Ⓡ *Stickies.* If the brake shoes are slow to grab the rim and slow to release it, and the handle and cable are both OK, then the mechanism must be rusty, mud-clogged, or broken inside. If there is some lubricant handy, squirt a drop on each pivot bolt. Then try grabbing a cantilever or brake arm with each hand and rocking them back and forth a bunch. Take the wheel off the bike and repeat the rocking action if you need to (just don't push so hard on the canti-levers/brake arms that you break the springs or the mecha-nisms). Try loosening the pivot bolt, resetting the spring, and retightening the pivot bolt, as described in the **One-shoe drag** section, above. When you have the brake working passably, ride home and do an overhaul there, as described below.

Ⓜ Ⓡ *Brake mechanism overhaul.* To overhaul your brake mechanism, all you really do is take each cantilever or brake arm off the mount (the pole thing that it pivots on), then clean and lube the parts, replace any that are ruined or rusty, and put the cantilever or arm back on the bike.

Ⓜ Ⓡ Start by undoing the brake cable. Mountain bikers, take the removable end of the transverse cable out of its slot at the end of one cantilever or brake arm. It's a good idea to leave the anchor bolt tight—you don't need to move the cantilever very far to overhaul it. Roadies, undo the cable anchor bolt.

Ⓜ When the cable is loose, use an Allen key to loosen (c-cl) the pivot bolt of one of the brake arms. It may be a bit difficult to turn even after the first twist or two; folks often use thread locking compound (like Loctite) on brake pivot bolts. When the bolt is all the way out, slide the can-tilever arm off the mount, observing which hole in the mount plate the end of the spring is stuck into.

Ⓡ When the cable is loose, loosen (c-cl) and remove the locknut and adjusting nut at the end of the pivot bolt, then remove the brake arms. Clean them and replace if necessary. See Illustration 2-11 to identify all those little parts. Rebuild the mechanism the way it came apart, then adjust the adjusting nut so it works smoothly, hold the adjusting nut still with one wrench, and tighten (cl) the locknut with another.

M Turn the cantilever unit face down, so the end of the spring that was in the mount-plate hole is pointing up at you. Check the brass surface of the hole in the cantilever that pivots on the mount. This surface, called a bushing, should be perfectly clean, smooth, greased, and rust-free. If it isn't, clean it with a cotton swab or corner of a rag, then smooth it with fine-grade emery paper or sandpaper wrapped around the mounting bolt or a Phillips screwdriver or something. Replace the cantilever if the bushing is too funky to save. Check the mount for a smooth, clean, rust-free condition, too. Being steel, it is more susceptible to rust. When both the mount and the cantilever bushing are smooth and clean, put grease on the mount.

M Next check the spring to see if either end is bent cockeyed; if the spring is bent, or if you have had lots of trouble with one-shoe drag and the bike is old, replace the spring AND its mate in the other cantilever, so you have a strong, well-matched pair. (Ah, what a concept!)

M When all the parts are replaced or clean, smooth, and lubed, make sure the spring is pushed into the cantilever so the hidden end of it is in the socket down in there, then slide the cantilever back onto the mount, making sure the visible end of the spring goes into the same hole in the mount plate that it came out of. If your brakes are kind of slow to release, you can put the spring end in a *higher* hole in the mount plate, as long as you make a mental note to do the same thing with the spring in the other cantilever, so the two are balanced.

M When you have overhauled and remounted both cantilevers, push the brake shoes into the rim by hand and hook the removable end of the transverse cable back into its slot and ride in peace; you'll be able to stop when you need to stop, and your brakes will release when you want to go.

M R What's that? One-shoe drag problems? Oh dear. This sometimes happens after an overhaul, even if you *did* put the spring ends into the right holes in the mount plates; see the **One-shoe drag** section in this chapter.

M R *Brake shoe cockeyed.* You banged your brake or it rattled loose, so one of the brake shoes hits the rim crosswise or not at all. Fix it quick, before it wears a hole in the tire or gets caught in the spokes. You have to loosen (c-cl) the nut on the mounting bolt that holds the shoe to the rest of the mechanism (if it isn't already loose), then move the brake shoe around until you can see that it's lined up so it'll squeeze exactly on the middle of the wall of the wheel rim. It should look exactly like the one on the other side, so the two grab the rim at the same angle.

M Now, although the concept of lining up a brake shoe to mirror its mate sounds simple, in practice it can be as complex as family relationship dynamics. First you must make sure that the shoe is at the same level in its groove in the cantilever as its partner (they've gotta be coming from the same *place*, OK?). Then make sure the poles that hold the shoes are lined up at the same angle, and if possible, set the poles so equal amounts of them are sticking out from the cantilevers toward the rim, as shown in Illustration 2-8. As if that isn't enough, you must also make sure the brake shoe you're aligning has a SLIGHT toe-in, so that when you look down on it from above, the end of the brake shoe that is toward the front of the bike is slightly closer to the wheel rim than the trailing edge of the brake shoe. Now, that's a *lot* to get right all at once. If you're at home, you can make the job a lot easier by taking the wheel off the bike, taking the tire and tube off the wheel, then replacing the tire-less wheel on the bike so you can align the brake shoes without having the tire blocking your view.

M When you finally get the brake shoe lined up, hold it there firmly with one hand while you tighten (cl) the mounting bolt. Take it easy on that bolt; they strip easily.

M R *Brake shoes worn or slipping.* If your brakes don't seem to work well and the shoes are worn down, don't panic. Worn brake shoes can often work as well or better than new ones, if the brake system is adjusted and you use the brakes wisely. The first step to fix the brakes is to adjust them, as described in the *Brake Cables* section, above.

M R If your brakes are slipping because they are wet, all you have to do is *think ahead* about your braking, and put the brakes on lightly for a few seconds to whisk the water off both the rim and the brake shoes, so the brakes will stop you when you need them. This technique will almost always keep the brakes from slipping and then grabbing in that terrifying way that wet brakes do.

M R If your brakes are slipping from overuse and over-heating on long, hot, steep descents, use them *intermittently* so they don't get so hot and glazed. If the hill is so steep that you need to use the brakes almost all the time, alternate your use of the front and rear brakes. You may have to stop and let them cool, or cool the rims off in the water at a creek crossing. Whatever you do, avoid the nervous tendency to leave both brakes on lightly as you descend. That just burns 'em up.

M R If your brake shoes really are worn all the way down to bare metal, here's a last-ditch trick to get you home. See if there is a leftover ledge of brake shoe rubber that protrudes under the edge of the rim when you put the brakes

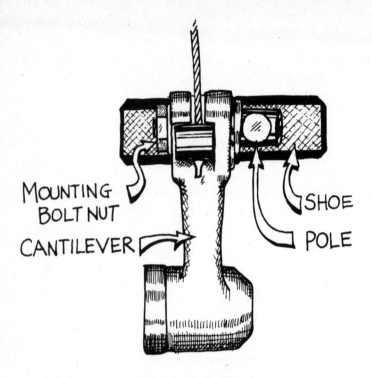

2-12 Brake Shoe

on. If there is a ledge like that, take a pocket knife and cut the thinnest outer edge of it off. CAREFUL: it's easy to poke a hole in the tire as you do this. Then loosen (c-cl) the bolt that holds the shoe to the brake mechanism and shift the shoe alignment up so the new braking surface you have just made hits the middle of the rim wall. Tighten (cl) the mounting bolt while holding the brake shoe in its new position. Try out the brake to see if you have increased your stopping power. It won't be up to snuff, but it'll get you home if you take it easy. If the worn shoes wind up cockeyed, so they aren't hitting the middle of the rim walls, see **brake shoe cockeyed**, above. Whatever you do, install new brake shoes before your next ride.

M R *Brake shoes squeaking or juddering.* When you apply the brakes, your whole bike vibrates, and, if you're going fast, your brakes screech like a Model T with its original equipment. Don't let this bother you as long as the brakes stop you smoothly. If they are so juddery you can't make controlled stops, first check to make sure the rims of your wheels are clean, and the cantilevers or brake arms are mounted tight to the frame.

M R If your front brake is juddering badly, check the headset to make sure the bearings are adjusted right. Then check the brake shoe alignment. Get your head over the brakes and peer down past the tire at each shoe as you apply and release the brakes. Does the back end of either rubber brake shoe hit the rim before the front end? If it does, it will squeal or judder. On many cantilever brakes, you can loosen the mounting bolt and adjust the toe-in as well as the vertical and horizontal alignment of the brake shoe. You may have to twist a beveled (wedge-shaped) washer around the brake shoe mounting bolt, or shift the mounting bolt and some cupped washers to toe the shoe in properly. If you can't get the brake shoes toed in right with gentle efforts, don't fight them. Use the brakes sparingly to reduce your squeaking or judder problem on your way home. Then you may need to replace the shoes, the cantilevers (if they are cheapo ones that are loose and flobby on the mounts), or (if a front wheel is juddering badly) even the *fork* to solve your problem. Front wheel judder or fork flutter can be due to a combination of poorly aligned brake shoes, anodized or grutty/glazed rims, and a fork with too much fore-and-aft flexibility built into it.

Coaster Brake

C To ***overhaul a coaster-brake hub,*** first take the rear wheel off the bike. See page 96 if you need help doing this job. If taking the wheel off seemed like a huge hassle to you, consider taking your brake problem to a good bike shop. If taking the wheel off was easy and got you all curious about what kind of a spiffy mechanical puzzle you were going to find inside the hub, then you are probably what they call "mechanically inclined" and you'll probably do fine on this overhaul yourself.

C Before you start wildly unscrewing all the things that keep the guts of the hub inside there, though, pause a sec, clean up your work area, clean the hub off, and figure out a way to hold the wheel still while you're working on it. A brake hub has quite a few little parts in it, and if they get dirty or out of order before you put them all back together, the hub will not work right later.

C So, start by cleaning all dirt and gunk off the outside of the hub. If you've been out riding in the swamps or cruising the sand dunes, it may even make sense to take the wheel to a do-it-yourself car wash and blast the gunk off with a hot water jet. Then take a stiff wire brush and clean out the threads of the axle ends as well as you can. This will make all the threading on and threading off of small hub parts easier during the overhaul.

C Next, lock the brake arm tightly in place on its end of the axle. This is done by holding the arm still with one hand and getting a wrench that fits snug on the locknut, then tightening (cl) that locknut hard against the brake arm. If the locknut is just a thin one, unscrew (c-cl) the axle nut, get about four thick washers that will fit around the axle, then tighten (cl) the axle nut back down, so it can help hold that brake arm tightly in place.

◨ Now hold the wheel flat, so the brake arm end of the axle is sticking straight down, and clamp the nut that is at the lower end of the axle in a vise. You got no vises? Good for you. A C-clamp will do the trick. Just hold the wheel flat at the corner of a table, so the brake arm end of the axle is sticking straight down past the corner, and the brake arm itself is resting *on* the corner of the table. Then clamp the brake arm firmly with a C-clamp. If you not only have a vise, but a slick two-hole, axle-vise tool, you can just stick the end of the axle into the big hole of the vise tool and tighten the vise up on it.

◨ OK, one way or the other you have your wheel held in place horizontally, with the end of the axle that *doesn't* have the brake arm sticking *up*. That's how things are arranged in Illustration 2-13. Take the axle nut off (c-cl) that upper end of the axle, holding onto the wheel and brake arm with your free hand to keep things still. The axle should not spin, even if the threads on it are a bit rough. If the axle does spin when you turn the nut, you haven't locked the nuts on the other end tight enough. Go back and do that over.

◨ Put the axle nut down on a clean rag on your workbench or table or whatever, at one end of the rag, so you can line all the other brake parts up next to it as you take them off. If there is a serrated washer under the nut you just took off, take off the washer and place it next to the nut, with the bumps down, just like they were when the washer was around the axle. That way, when you go to put the washer back on the axle, you won't have to wonder which way is right-side up.

◨ Next look closely at the sprocket and the shiny dust cap that is just under it. Do they look OK? No bent or chipped teeth on the sprocket? No cracks or bent-out places on the dust cap? Is the ring spring tight in its groove? If those things are all OK, and your chain hasn't been skipping due to the sprocket being extremely old and worn down, then skip the next two paragraphs and get on with the brake overhaul.

C If your sprocket or dust cap is shot, you have to take the sprocket off. Get a skinny-ended screwdriver and stick it between the ring spring and the fat driver it is stretched around; there are little crescent-shaped gaps cut into the side of the driver where your skinny screwdriver tip will fit easily. Pry one end of the ring spring out from the driver, then move on to the next gap, so the spring will work its way out of the groove from one end to the other. Hold your free hand above the spring, like a shield wrapped around the end of the axle, so the spring can't leap up and poke your eye out, or fly across the garage and roll down the driveway headed for the land of never-never.

C When the spring is off, take off the sprocket and the dust cap, and place them on your clean rag, with the same side facing up that was facing up on the wheel. Get the replacement parts you need, making sure they are exactly the same as the originals, and put the dust cap, sprocket, and ring spring back around the driver just the way they were before. Make sure the sprocket is "dished" the same way it was before. Wonder how you get that ring spring stretched on there? Just start one end in the groove, then work your way around the spring from that end, holding the other end of the spring down and prying with the skinny screwdriver at each little crescent-shaped gap so the spring stretches out and around that fat driver.

C To proceed with the brake overhaul, loosen (c-cl) the locknut (that's the next thing in line on the axle.) Take it off, and put it in line on your clean rag. Loosen (c-cl) the threaded cone that's next on the axle, and put it next in line on the rag.

C Next lift out the retainer of ball bearings. (If there is a thin dust cap holding them in, pry that out very carefully with a screwdriver, working around and around the ring as

AXLE NUT

LOCK NUT

THREADED CONE

SMALL BEARING
RETAINER

RING SPRING

SPROCKET

DUST COVER

DRIVER

HELIX THREAD

BIG BEARING
RETAINER

HUB SHELL

HELIX THREAD

CLUTCH CONE

BRAKE SHOES

CLUTCH SPRING

CLAMP
HERE

AXLE

BRAKE CONE

BRAKE ARM

LOCK NUT

AXLE NUT

2-13 Coaster-Brake Hub

you pry, to keep the little thing from getting bent.) When you get the retainer full of ball bearings out of the hub, put it right down on the clean rag, with the same side of the ring up that was up when the retainer was in place. Say, you're making a pretty professional-looking row of parts on your clean rag! Keep things straight like that, and you'll get a rewarding feeling when you put the wheel all back together and it works perfectly, with no parts left over.

🄲 The next thing to take out of the hub is the driver and sprocket assembly. Hold the wheel hub down against the brake-arm end of the axle and turn the sprocket slowly (c-cl); it will spin right up out of the hub on its large helix threads. Set the whole assembly down on the clean rag, lift the large bearing retainer ring out of the hub shell, and put it down by the driver assembly.

🄲 Still holding the wheel in place? Good. Now lift it with one hand, slowly, and catch any loose brake parts that slip out around the brake arm as the rising hub shell clears them. On the type of hub illustrated, two or three brake shoes may come slipping down out of the hub. On other brakes, four little shoes might come tumbling out, or you may find that there is a whole stack of thin brake discs around the axle. That's OK, just catch any brake shoes that do fall, and put them in a line on the clean rag.

🄲 Set the wheel aside, then slide the clutch cone up off the axle and put it in order on the clean rag. On different brakes there are clutch cones of all sizes and shapes, but they all have the big helix threads inside them, and they all pull the clutch tight when you pedal forward, and push over against the brake shoes or discs when you backpedal. You may want to put the driver and the clutch cone together right now, threading helix to helix (cl), so you can figure out for yourself how the whole hub works. Get the idea? Isn't it slick?

◉ After you've put the driver and clutch cone down on the clean rag, the only things left on the axle that you can take off are the clutch spring, and maybe (on some brake types) a pile of brake discs or a single brake spring washer.

◉ Clean all of the parts, one at a time, including the bearings still on the brake cone, and the inside of the hub shell. Replace the clutch spring no matter what problem you had with your brakes. If your hub has both a clutch and a brake shoe spring, replace both of them.

◉ Then check the helix threads of the driver and clutch cone to make sure they aren't chipped or worn away. Check the brake shoes to make sure they aren't worn smooth on the outer surfaces, bent, or marred by a little burr somewhere on the braking surface. If you have brake discs, see that they aren't burred or glazed over with old, dry grease. Check the inside of the brake hub to make sure it isn't all scored or marred by burrs. All those brake surfaces have to be perfect for the brakes to work right.

◉ Take a steel ruler and line its edge up with the axle to make sure the axle isn't bent. Look closely at the bearing dust caps and make sure none of them are bent. Check the bearings to make sure they aren't pitted or worn flat.

◉ Replace any parts that are wrecked. You may want to draw a little picture of any part you have to take to a shop; leave the picture of the part right in the place where the part went on your clean rag line-up, so you won't forget how to set the thing back in place for quick reassembly.

◉ OK, got all the new parts you need? Bet it was a pain finding them, wasn't it? And a shock to learn how much they charge for some of those simple little things. Such is life.

◉ Clean all the parts again, new and old, including the brake arm and cone assembly that are still attached to the axle. Use a safe but strong solvent for gunk removal, and after each part is clean make sure it *stays* clean until it is safely back inside the hub. A bit of grit in the wrong place inside a brake hub can totally ruin the thing. If the hub gets ruined, you'll have to go through this whole process AGAIN. You wouldn't want to do that, now, would you? So get anal.

C Start the ***brake hub reassembly*** by spreading a bunch of good multi-use grease (beware: Some types of bike grease will glaze over at the high temperatures that build up inside a brake hub) on the bearings that are on the brake cone you left locked in place on the axle. Then put your NEW clutch spring in place.

C Next you have to grease the brake shoes (or discs), hold them in place around the brake cone, slide the clutch cone down the axle until it nestles against the brake shoes, and finally slide the wheel over the whole business. This can be tricky. Use lotsa grease on the brake shoes, and they may stay in place while you slide the wheel down over them.

C You may even have to take the axle out of whatever device is holding it, turn the axle horizontal, then hold the brake shoes in place and slide the hub over them. However you do the trick, make sure the shoes wind up snug against the fixed brake cone, and lined up with the "key" bumps and the slanting faces of both the brake and clutch cones, so the brake shoes stay in place when the wheel is whirling around them. When you get the hub resting down flush on its bearings, hold it against them and turn it, peering down into the hub at the brake shoes as you do so. Brake shoes snug down against that fixed brake cone? Wheel sliding around them without any hang-ups? Good.

C The wheel will wobble and wiggle as you turn it on just that single set of bearings, of course, but the brake shoes shouldn't flop around down in there, or get jammed cattywampus against the turning hub shell.

■ When you're sure you have the brake parts lined up right inside the wheel, put the big retainer of bearings into its race in the hub shell, grease the bearings, and turn (cl) the driver assembly down into the clutch cone on its helix threads until it rests against the bearings.

■ Next put the small retainer of bearings into the race on top of the driver assembly, grease them, and spin (cl) the cone down the axle until it is snug against the bearings. Back it off a bit (c-cl), hold it with one hand, and use the other hand to turn the sprocket (cl) as it would turn if you were pedaling the bike. Turn the sprocket, hold it still and let the wheel coast, then turn the sprocket the other way (c-cl), as if you were backpedaling.

■ Do you feel a nice smooth application of the brakes? Does the wheel slow quickly and quietly to a stop? If not, take the cone, bearings, and driver assembly off the axle, and take the wheel off if you have to, in order to get those brake shoes and their cones in line so they coast and brake like they're supposed to.

■ If you can't get it together so it works when you put all the stuff on the upper end of the axle, take the wheel to a pro and ask him or her if you can watch the thing being put together so it will work. That way you'll learn the tricks, and you won't be afraid to take the thing on again if you have to later.

■ When the brake is working smoothly, tighten (cl) the threaded cone again by hand, then back it off about a quarter turn, or until you can just *barely* feel some play if you wiggle the rim of the wheel gently with your fingertips. Turn (cl) the locknut onto the axle and tighten (cl) it against the threaded cone. Try to get hold of a cone wrench that's big enough to fit the cone and hold it still while you tighten the locknut, so you can be sure the hub will keep the precise adjustment you have just given it. If the hub gets too tight, you can ruin the bearings. If it's too loose, the axle may bend or the driver may fatigue and snap. So get it right.

■ Take the wheel out of the vise or whatever was holding it, then put the washers (if you have any) on both ends of the axles (serrated bumps facing IN, remember) and thread the axle nuts on (cl).

■ Put the wheel on the bike, turning to page 108 if you need any hints. Then air up the tire and ride in peace. You've got good brakes again!

CHAPTER 3

Handlebars and Stem

DESCRIPTION: Ⓜ Mountain bikes often have almost straight handlebars, and the bars are often held by one or more binder bolts in a custom chrome-moly steel tube stem. The handlebars may have bar ends attached by binder or expander bolts.

Ⓡ The curved-down drop bars are most common on road bikes. Typically, they are held in a slick, smooth, aluminum stem by a binder bolt, which is often hidden from view. You can add a clip-on aerodynamic bar to your drop bars, but the resultant riding position is pretty unstable. Not worth the danger unless you are a time trialist or triathelete. By the way, the faddish, upside-down position for drop bars is also unsafe. It invites impalement. You like it? You can have it.

C Most cruisers have all-rounder-type bars, which are close to flat, but are curved near the ends so the grips aim more toward the back of the bike. The stems on cruisers are usually inexpensive versions of the stems used for road bikes.

DIAGNOSIS: C R M For some reason, people often get confused about just what holds what in place on the handlebars and stem. The following symptoms tell you what part of the setup is loose.

C R M If the handlebars swivel up and down, so you can twist them in the stem, then your problem is a ***loose binder bolt***. If the bars are loose in relation to the front wheel, so they tend to aim off to one side or the other when you are riding straight ahead, the problem is a ***loose or cockeyed stem.*** If you have a bar end that is loose, all you have to do is line up the loose bar end with the other one, then tighten (cl) the mounting bolt that squeezes the bar end around the end of your handlebar, or the expander that goes in the end of the bar. If your handlebars are too high or too low, this also requires working on the *stem*, not the headset as you might suspect. One exception to this rule is the type of stem that works as a locknut for the headset. You *can't* adjust the bar height with that kind of stem. To raise the handlebars, you have to buy a taller or more upright-angled stem.

C R M No matter what you're doing to either your handlebar or stem, check to see that the tips of the handlebars or bar ends are plugged. If they aren't, plug them immediately—before you get back on the bike and start riding. If you don't have official bar plugs with you, use a wine or champagne cork, or even a short piece of stick with the end rounded off. Bare bar tips can gore you if you fall on them. I know this from experience.

PROBLEMS: C R M *Loose binder bolt.* Tighten (cl) the bolt with an Allen key (usually 5 or 6 mm). Some beefy stems have two or even four binderbolts; tighten (cl) them all evenly, turning each a bit at a time.

C R M If your bars slip because they are simply too small in diameter for your stem, loosen (c-cl) the binder bolt as much as possible, then find a smooth, uncrumpled aluminum beer or pop can (all too easy to find on many backroads and trails). Cut out a 3-inch by 2½-inch strip of the side of the can with a sharp knife, being careful not to bend or kink the metal. Use the strip you cut out as a shim, wrapped around the bulged central portion of the bars where they fit inside the stem. Tighten (cl) the binderbolt as well as you can, and, when you get home, replace the bars or stem to get a better fit.

C R M *Loose or cockeyed stem.* To straighten bars that have gotten cockeyed, stand in front of the bike and hold the front wheel between your legs (you don't have to get weird with it, just hold it still). Grasp the handlebars firmly with both hands and straighten them so the stem extension lines up with the front wheel and the bars run straight across, perpendicular to the line of travel of the front wheel. If the bars won't budge, on most stems you loosen (c-cl) the expander bolt, using an Allen key, then tap the head of the bolt with a hammer, rock, or something, to unwedge the stem so it can be straightened.

M If you have one of those stems that acts as a locknut for your headset, it has *binder* bolts instead of an expander bolt, as shown in Illustration 3-2. Loosen (c-cl) the binder bolts if you need more looseness to move the stem. DON'T loosen the Allen bolt at the top of the stem where most stems have their expander bolts; LEAVE THAT BOLT ALONE. Just loosen (c-cl) the binder bolts, then adjust the bars so they're straight.

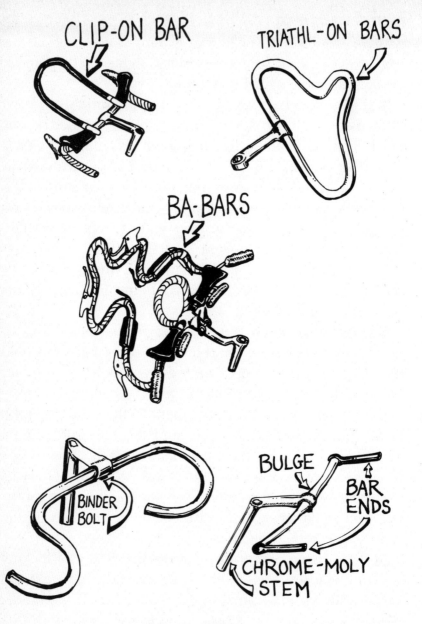

CLIP-ON BAR

TRIATHL-ON BARS

BA-BARS

BINDER BOLT

BULGE

BAR ENDS

CHROME-MOLY STEM

3-1 Handlebars

C R M Once your stem and handlebars are straight, tighten (cl) the stem expander bolt (binder bolts, you fancy stem

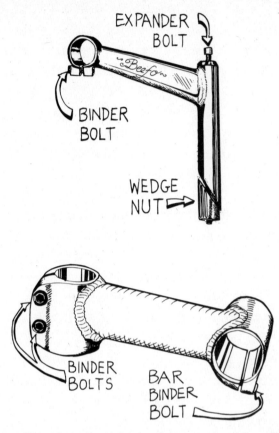

3-2 Top: Standard Stem; Bottom: Locknut Stem

people) enough so the stem will stay put, but no tighter. Try twisting the bars again. If they stay put unless you pull quite hard to one side, the expander bolt is tight enough. It should not be so tight that the stem can't slip in case of a crash. If you fall on the bars, you want *them* to give, not you.

C R M *Stem creaky, cracked, or broken.* When you ride up hills and pull hard on the handlebars, your stem creaks. First check to see that it isn't loose; tighten (cl) the expander bolt as described in the previous section. Also check to make sure the shaft of the stem, where it binds to the steering column that comes up from the fork, is well greased. Grease on the threads of all binder and expander bolts is a must, too. Then check for cracks on the stem, and look closely to see if it is the correct diameter; it should just barely slip down into the fork column in the headset.

C R M If you find any signs of cracks on the stem, especially at a joint or near the binder bolt, ride home gingerly, without pulling up hard or leaning down hard on the bars. If your stem is broken and you're miles from help, here's an emergency fix. Undo the front brake (undo the transverse cable so it won't catch on the knobbies), tie or balance the bars on what's left of the stem, then ride home holding the stump of the stem, pulling on the rear brake cable where it runs bare along the top tube in order to stop. If you have no exposed section of cable running to your rear brake, you have to steer with one hand on the stem stump while you squeeze the brake lever with the other hand. Verrry tricky. Proceed with due caution.

C R M When you get home, use the **handlebars broken** procedure to take the bars off the bike, then replace the stem and put the bars back in, as described at the end of the broken handlebar procedure.

C R M *Handlebars too high or low.* To adjust the height of the handlebars if you have a standard stem, you have to loosen (c-cl) the expander bolt a couple of turns with an Allen key, then tap on the head of the bolt with something heavy like a rock or a hard piece of wood. A short piece of 2-by-4 with a knot at one end works fine. When the expander bolt is unwedged, undo the front brake transverse cable, then lower or raise the handlebars. Tighten (cl) the expander bolt as explained in *loose or cockeyed stem,* above. If you need to readjust the front brake, see PROBLEMS in the *Brake Cables* section.

M If you have one of the fancy stems that acts as a locknut for the headset, you can't adjust the height of it. You have to buy a new stem that is taller or that has a more upright angle. Seems like a fairly expensive and labor-intensive way to adjust your bar height, no?

R ***Drop bar bent in.*** You've taken a spill? You are scraped and shook up, but OK. The bike is OK too, except that one of the handlebars has a new bend in it, so that it toes in. When you stop shaking, put the bike on its side so that the still-straight bar is flat on the ground. Step on the drop portion of the straight bar (careful, don't break the brake lever) and pull firmly upward on the folded bar. If the bars are aluminum, you might be able to get them straight enough to ride. Steel bars are a lot harder to bend. And any bar that has been bent and unbent is weak, so when you get a chance, get a replacement.

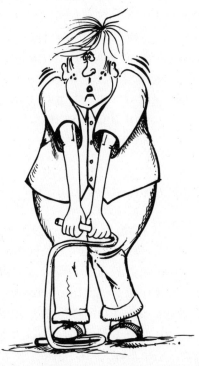

3-3 Straightening a Bent Drop Bar

C R M *Handlebars broken; replacement.* First get any grip, tape, brake levers, bar ends, horn, or whatever off the old ones. If you have lots of trouble removing old hand-grips, take the bike to a bike shop or garage, ask them if you can use the cleaning nozzle on their shop air hose, then stick the nozzle in the hole at the end of one hand-grip, put your thumb over the hole in the other grip, and blast air pressure into the handlebars. Nine times out of ten the grips will both come loose and slide right off. For that tenth tough grip, use a razor knife and lotsa care to cut it off. Then loosen (c-cl) the binder bolt completely. Slide the bars out and take them to a shop. Get some that are the same diameter at the stem or a little smaller. If you get smaller ones, buy the correct size shim to make the new bars fit the stem. Don't get bars that are much too big for your stem—they will stretch and weaken the stem.

C R M If the bars are just a hair too big, you can do a neat trick to open up the stem if you have the kind of binder bolt that screws into a threaded hole. Take the binder bolt all the way out, turn it into the threaded hole from the back side, stick a penny into the slot there, and tighten (cl) the backward binder bolt up against the penny to spread the stem opening a little.

R *Tape worn or unwound.* Take the plugs out of the ends of the bars. If there is a screw in the middle of the plug, unscrew (c-cl) it until it is loose, then push it in and work the plug out. If your plugs don't have screws, just yank them out. Unwind the old tape completely. Get new tape. I recommend either cloth, thin leather, or the rubbery, stretchy type of plastic tape that is thicker in the middle than at the edges. You can use the extra-thick tape, or you can put on several layers of standard tape for a softer feel on your bars, but the cushiness can get to the point where you are out of touch with that zingy responsiveness of your

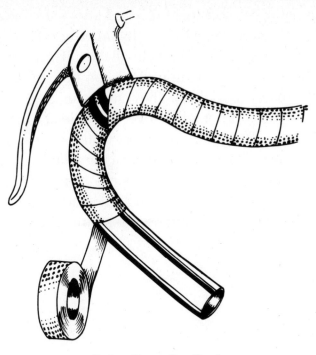

3-4   Drop-Bar Taping

bike's front end. Start wrapping the tape about 3 inches out
from the mid-point of the bar where it is held by the stem.
If the tape has no gum on it, you can stick the end down
with a little piece of Scotch tape. Whichever type of tape
you use, start by wrapping a couple turns in one place to
cover the tape end. As you lay the tape on, keep it tight, and
make it go directly from the roll to the bar. There's less to
get tangled up that way. Overlap at least a third of the tape's
width at all points. At the bends, you have to overlap more
on the inside than on the outside. Just make sure it overlaps
enough on the outside of the bend.

▣ Angle the tape across the bar behind the hand lever,
making sure it is tight all the time. (See Illustration 3-4.) You
can fold the hood up on most hand levers, so you can wrap
tape close around the lever's post. At the end of the bar,
leave a little tape to tuck in under the plug. When you've

finished taping and tucking, push and knock the plug back in with your hands. Don't use a hammer; it will mash the tape in two and you'll have to start all over. If you have tape left over, you can wrap it around the top tube of the frame where the handlebars hit if they are swung all the way around. Or you can put a little over the hole at the top end of your seat post, if you have a post with a hole at the top. Or you can use a little on a leaky vacuum cleaner hose, or a noisy kid's mouth, or a cracked pump handle. Sometimes I feel like my whole mish-mosh life is held together by scraps of handlebar tape and used bike inner tubes.

CHAPTER 4

Headset

DESCRIPTION AND DIAGNOSIS: 🄲 🅁 🄼 The headset is the set of bearings that holds your front fork to the rest of the bike frame and allows the front wheel to steer. The steering column at the top of the fork goes up through the head tube of the frame, and all of those bearing parts (see Illustrations 4-1 and 4-2) of the headset go around the fork tube. There may be some variation of parts on your headset, such as a special lockring with Allen set-screws, or seals on the bearing races, or interlocking teeth on the washer and the top threaded race, but the general layout will be the same.

🄼 Most mountain bikes have a stem that slides over the top end of the steering column and acts as a locknut. These bikes have a top race that is not threaded, as shown in Illustration 4-1. The locknut/stem makes it easy to remove your fork, which is nice if you have a shock fork and need to remove it for lubrication and overhaul. Threadless headsets also make for a much more reliable interface between the stem and the steering column.

C R M If your steering action gets unresponsive, or you hear clanks or grackly crunchy noises and feel looseness in your front end as you go over bumps, your headset is probably loose. Lift the front wheel off the ground a few inches and drop it; if you hear a clank, the headset is loose for sure. To test for more subtle headset looseness, apply the front brake fully, push down on the handlebars, and rock the bike forward and back. Can you feel a sort of slippy-shifty looseness or see that the front fork is shifting back and forth in relation to the frame? These symptoms indicate a loose headset, too. Just to make sure the problem is with the headset and not the fork (especially a shock fork) or the wheel, rest the front wheel on the ground and try to wiggle the tire from side to side; if the fork slops and wiggles side to side, your shocks are shot (see page 90); if the wheel wiggles, you may have loose front wheel bearings or a wheel that is loose in the fork. For either of these problems, see the Hub PROBLEMS section on page 114.

C R M If your steering action becomes rough or sticky, and you notice that the bike is a little hard to balance when you are going slow, the problem is probably that the headset is stiff.

PROBLEMS: C R M *Headset loose.* If you have noticed a clanky or wandering front end and used the diagnostic tests above to determine that your headset is loose, here is the way to snug it up.

C R M First see if you can turn the big top locknut counterclockwise a turn or two to loosen it. Try doing it by hand. If it has Allen screws set into the sides of it, holding it tightly in place, loosen (c-cl) those with an Allen key, then loosen (c-cl) the locknut. If you have a stem/locknut unit, see the headset loose procedure on page 81.

C R M After you have loosened the locknut, tighten (cl) the top threaded race by hand. If the headset is loose, you

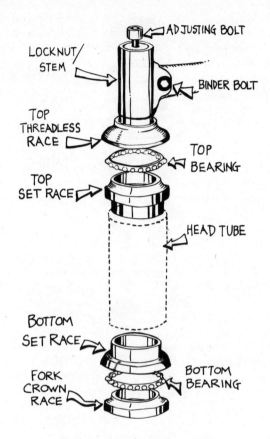

ADJUSTING BOLT

LOCKNUT/
STEM

BINDER BOLT

TOP
THREADLESS
RACE

TOP
BEARING

TOP
SET RACE

HEAD TUBE

BOTTOM
SET RACE

FORK
CROWN
RACE

BOTTOM
BEARING

4-1 Threadless Headset

should be able to do this easily. You can often do it even if you couldn't manage to loosen the locknut. When you have the threaded race as tight as possible, apply the front brake and rock the bike forward and back to see if there's still any looseness lurking in there. If so, tighten the threaded race some more, rocking the bike to and fro or turning the handlebars as you tighten, to make sure you are snugging up the race on the bearings as much as possible. When the headset is snug, tighten (cl) the locknut down by hand, too. If you have the proper wrench for your headset locknut, tighten the locknut thoroughly. If you are out in the open

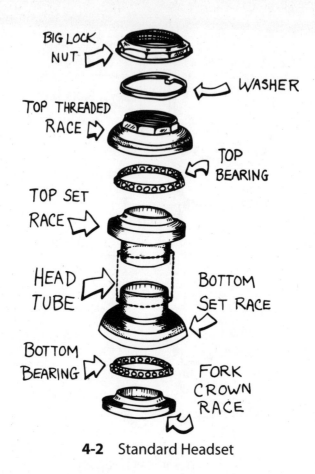

BIG LOCK NUT

WASHER

TOP THREADED RACE

TOP BEARING

TOP SET RACE

HEAD TUBE

BOTTOM SET RACE

BOTTOM BEARING

FORK CROWN RACE

4-2   Standard Headset

country and don't have a tool, just hand-tighten the locknut. That will hold it there for a while. If you go over a lot of rough terrain, you may have to retighten the headset by hand again before you get home. When you do get home, don't forget to adjust the thing carefully again, then tighten the locknut very thoroughly with the proper wrench.

C R M You may even need two wrenches, one to hold the threaded race still, and the other to tighten (cl) the top locknut. A big channel lock wrench and a huge crescent wrench will work if you don't have proper headset wrenches. If you have a lot of trouble with the tools you've gotten hold of, don't knock yourself out or mash up the threaded race or the big top locknut in the process. Take the bike to a good shop. They will have the right tools to do the job. Also, if the headset is an aluminum one, you might want to replace it with a steel headset. Aluminum headsets have a reputation for looseness (tsk, tsk).

Ⓜ *Threadless headset loose.* All you have to do is loosen (c-cl) the binder bolts that cinch the stem onto the top of the steering column, then *gently* tighten the adjusting Allen bolt at the top of the stem. CAREFUL: it's easy to over-tighten it and mess up the plastic cap or the springy spider-nut that are pulled towards each other by that adjusting Allen bolt; all you want to do is snug the stem down on the bearings. Rock the bike forward and back gently with your weight on the bars to test for looseness. When the headset is snug, tighten (cl) the binder bolts thoroughly, and you're set to go.

Ⓒ Ⓡ Ⓜ *Headset tight.* Either the bearings are dry or tight, or the steering column may be bent. Look at the front end of the bike from one side. Does the front wheel look cocked back further than it should be? Have you slammed into a log or rock lately? Taken a bad endo (flipped over the front)? Try steering the handlebars all the way to the right as far as they will go, and then all the way to the left. If the headset gets stiffer at either extreme, you can almost bet you have a bent steering column. They are hard to straighten, but if the bend is severe and your steering is really bad, see page 88 for a way to get the fork pulled out straight.

Ⓒ Ⓡ Ⓜ If the steering column is straight and the only problem is that the bearings are dry or dirty, get a bit of lubricant worked into the headset. Turn the bike upside down and squirt it in, using the little application tube if your lubricant comes with one. If the bearings aren't sealed, it's easier to lube them; I remember squeezing mayonnaise from one of those little packets you get at fast food places into my headset once. Worked like a charm for the rest of the ride. But if you do any stop-gap lubrication on a ride, make a mental note to do a complete overhaul of your headset when you get home, using proper bike grease and the procedure below to make sure you get it all right.

C R M If a standard headset is just too tight, you have to try to loosen (c-cl) the top locknut, then loosen (c-cl) the top threaded race just a bit (one-eighth of a turn or less), then tighten (cl) the top locknut. You need a headset spanner to do this properly; the one you get with a Cool Tool will work if the top locknut isn't really tight. If it is really tight, you may have to struggle along with your stiff steering until you can get to a farm or something, then borrow a big adjustable wrench to loosen and tighten your top locknut. Do adjust that tight headset as soon as you can, though; a tight headset feels horrible when you try to correct imbalance by steering, especially when you're picking your way through a slow, technical section of trail. If you don't believe this, just try riding no-handed with a tight headset.

C R M *Headset overhaul.* Start the overhaul by laying the bike down on its left side with a clean white rag under the headset. Remove the front wheel; see page 96 if you need help.

C R M If you have a standard stem, loosen (c-cl) the expander bolt that's on top of the stem two full turns, then tap the bolt head with a hammer to unwedge the stem inside the fork tube. Twist and pull the handlebars to get the stem out. If you have enough brake and gear cable slack, turn the handlebars to one side and lash one end to the down tube with an old inner tube or something. Remove the front wheel if you haven't already. Then loosen (c-cl) and remove the top locknut.

M If you have a locknut/stem type of headset, loosen (c-cl) the binder bolts on the stem, then hold the fork so it stays in the frame, as shown in Illustration 4-3, then loosen (c-cl) the adjusting Allen bolt that's on top of the stem, all the way, so you can take the stem off the top of the steering column.

C R M No matter what kind of stem you have, the next step is to either unscrew (c-cl) the top threaded race, or slide it up off the steering column if it isn't threaded. Then you can slide the steering column of the front fork out of the frame. Take the bearing rings off the races, observing carefully which side of the bearings has the solid ring. On almost all bikes, the bearings will be in retainer rings; if they aren't, take the loose balls out of the races and count them, NOW, so you'll know how many go back in there. After you have the bearings off the bike, check for thin little sealer rings that fit around the outer edges of the smaller bearing races in each bearing set. Take these sealer rings off carefully and note which way they fit around the races; they often

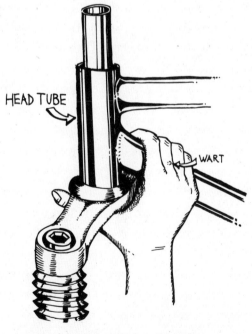

HEAD TUBE

WART

4-3 Holding Fork in Headset

have a special "stepped" profile so they fit around the edge of the race and stay put. You have to make sure you put them in the same way they came out.

C R M Clean all the bearing surfaces and the ball bearings with a soft, clean rag. Check the surfaces for pits, roughness, or cracks. Replace any bearing or race that is not shiny smooth. You may have to get help from a shop to remove and replace the set races or the fork crown race; they're often hammered tight into place, and you need special tools to get them off without bending them and/or damaging the frame tubes.

C R M When you have clean, smooth bearing parts, put some waterproof grease on the ball bearings, then put the lower bearings on the fork crown race, making sure you have the retaining ring for the ball bearings on the correct side (up or down) so it won't rub on the races. Slip the sealer ring around the race (if you have a sealer ring), and push the fork back into place in the frame. Then put the greased top set of ball bearings in place (add the sealer ring too, if you have one), and either turn (cl) or slide the top race onto the steering column.

C R M Now, if you have a standard stem, put your lock rings or washers back on the steering column, turn (cl) the top locknut down to them, then adjust the headset, as described in this chapter. When it's adjusted and the top locknut is tight, you can put the stem back in, line up the handlebars, and tighten (cl) the stem's expander bolt.

M If you have a locknut/stem headset, you have to hold the fork in place while you slide the locknut/stem unit onto the steering column. Then you *gently* tighten (cl) the adjusting bolt until the headset is snug. Then align the stem so the handlebars are straight in relation to the front wheel, and, finally, tighten (cl) the binder bolts.

CHAPTER 5

Frame and Fork

DESCRIPTION AND DIAGNOSIS: C R M The frame is more than it might seem. It is not just a lopsided diamond and two triangles of tubing stuck together somehow. It is the heart and soul of a bicycle. It is not just the most expensive part of the bike: it is the single most significant part in determining the quality of a bike. The fork is equally important. A great, lightweight fork can make all the difference in how a bike climbs, descends, and responds to the terrain. And the way that the frame and fork work together is critical, too.

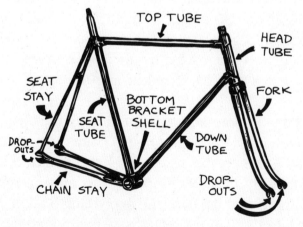

5-1 Frame

C R M The frame and fork are also the most difficult parts of your bike to repair. If you completely crumple any of the tubes of your frame, or if you smash the forks, or wear out the shocks when you are out in the middle of nowhere, you can't do much about it. If the bike is still rideable, ride it very gently; if not, walk. There are *some* tricks you can use—if a fork blade breaks, whittle a stick down to the right diameter, then jam it into one end of the blade and push the other end of the blade over the other end of the stick. But such frame and fork repairs are rarely workable. Trailside repairs on suspension-frame bicycles are even less likely to save you from a long walk home.

C R M Prevention is the best medicine for frame and fork problems; try to buy a really light, durable frame and fork to start with. Frame technology and suspension technology for shock forks and fully suspended bikes are changing constantly, but one rule of thumb you can always use is this: if a new-tech bike weighs more or is more prone to failure than a tried-and-proven, steel-tube bike, it's probably not worth spending extra money, time, and energy on. Whatever bike frame and fork you buy, respect their limitations by using good techniques going over and around obstacles. Good frames and forks don't usually break unless you are riding foolishly. No matter what anybody claims about certain shock forks or suspension frames, it is foolish to ride full-speed down a rocky mountainside unless you have spent a LOOOOONG time learning the art of high-speed descent.

C R M One note about *paint:* new frames usually have good paint jobs. Keep the original paint on a frame as long as possible. Keep the bike out of the rain and touch up scratches with auto touch-up paint to prevent rust. To repaint a frame you have to take everything off it. If you're up to that, use the various sections of this book that apply. If not, have a good shop do the job. Do-it-yourself painting

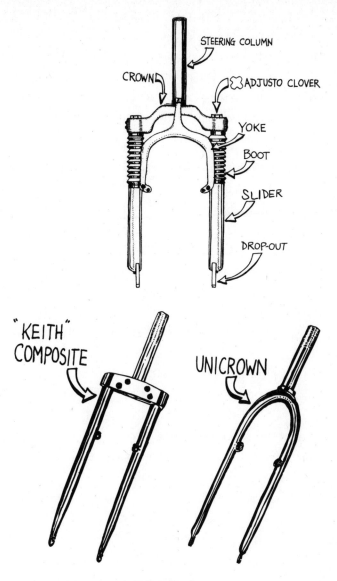

STEERING COLUMN

CROWN

ADJUSTO CLOVER

YOKE

BOOT

SLIDER

DROP-OUT

"KEITH" COMPOSITE

UNICROWN

5-2 Fork

means first thoroughly stripping the old paint (use a liquid paint remover and AVOID BREATHING THE FUMES). The frame has to be perfectly clean and dry. Then spray on a coat or two of primer, making each coat as smooth as possible and always letting it dry thoroughly before spraying the next coat. Then spray on several layers of epoxy paint. Or you can take the bare, prepared frame to an auto paint shop and get a bake-on job. You might get it done pretty cheaply if you're willing to have them put the frame through the works with an auto body. Just wait for one that has a color you like.

PROBLEMS: Ⓜ *Front end bent in.* So you hit a boulder. Or was it a log? Or was it that dip at the bottom of the gully that you thought you could pull the front end up out of, but you didn't *quite* make it? Oh, yes, it can happen to any of us, and *has* happened to many of us. The result is that either your fork or your down and top tubes are bent, or all three are bent, and now your front wheel hits the down tube so you can't ride home.

Ⓜ Try this last-ditch method of straightening the front end of your bike a bit; it won't make the bike perfect by any means, but it may get you home. My thanks to Cyclo-crosser Dan Nall for this trick; he showed me how to do it when we were *way* out in the woods, and a guy from Topanga "lunched out" in a rocky creek bed.

Ⓜ Have a friend hold the bike upright, or prop it against a post or a tree, and sit down on the ground with the front wheel between your thighs. I know that's a weird position, especially if your friend has a sadistic sense of humor, but you need to fix the thing, right? Push the pedals around with your toes until the right crank (the one with the chainrings) is pointing down and the left crank is pointing up. Place your left foot on the chainring, with your heel against the right crank, and place your right foot against the bottom bracket shell, with your toes up along the left crank, as shown in Illustration 5-3.

Ⓜ Now grab either the ends of the fork or the rim of the wheel where it is nearest to your chest. The taller you are,

5-3   Pulling Out the Front End

the easier it'll be to pull on the rim. If you are less than five feet tall, you may have to take the front wheel off so you can pull on the drop-outs at the ends of the fork.

M When you have a good grip on the rim or fork, first straighten your back (you'll strain it if it's curved), then try to hold the fork or wheel absolutely still with your hands as you push the bottom bracket and the rest of the bike away from you with your feet. Make your legs do the work, not your back and arms. If you have a light, unreinforced frame and fork, you may be amazed at how easily you can pull the front end of the bike out. Some super-heavy-duty frames and forks may be impossible to straighten using this method.

M If your fork is the only thing that is bent, and you have a really sturdy front end on your frame, you can try another straightening method; it is primitive, but if you are stuck out in the middle of nowhere, you may want to try it anyway. All you have to do is turn the front wheel all the way around backwards (you may have to undo the front brake and loosen the stem to do this), then put the front wheel against a tree and shove the bike from behind. Easy does it. I saw a desperate racer try this method once, only he sorta hurled the bike down against the ground on its reversed front wheel, and, instead of neatly straightening his front fork, he neatly crumpled both his top and down tubes, which neatly took him out of the race since the nearest spare bike was about five miles away.

M There are other ways to pull a front end out, like wedging the forks in the crotch of a tree and levering the frame back, but I think these methods have much more potential for ruining the bike than fixing it.

M Whatever you do to straighten things out, don't keep using your bent and straightened fork or frame. When you have limped home, take the fork or the whole frame to a first-rate bike shop and see if the thing can be accurately straightened by a pro framemaker, or if it should be replaced. And next time, use a bit more finesse to get over those rocks, logs, and holes at the bottoms of gullies.

M ***Shock forks squeaky.*** This can be due to worn parts, or it can be due to simple lack of lubricant, especially on elastomer-based suspension forks. For these forks, first adjust the forks to a loose setting if you can, then pull the boot off the upper part of the shock fork, dribble a light bicycle lubricant such as Tri-flow around the top of the lower tube, and work the fork vigorously a few times to get the lubricant down in there. If the squeakiness is related to looseness and fork flutter, take the fork to a good shop for overhaul.

M ***Fork flutter.*** When you put on the front brakes as you are flying down a bumpy single-track, the front end of your bike starts to waggle and jerk fore-and-aft under you. If you glance down (don't stare; you are flying down a hill, remember), you can see the fork flexing or fluttering fore-and-aft.

M The flutter takes on a rhythm all its own, which can throw off your judgment of obstacles ahead, and even throw you into an endo (over the bars), if the hill is steep and you have to put the brake on hard. The problem is a bad wave of vibration repeating itself in the fork. The harmonics from hell.

M If you have a shock fork, the flutter is probably a result of looseness due to wear and tear on the inner workings of the shock absorbing mechanism. Shocks are not made so you can take them apart and fix them yourself. Take your wobbly shock fork to a first-rate shop that repairs the brand and model you have, and be prepared to pay a tidy bundle for an overhaul.

M R Fork flutter on rigid forks is caused by brake shoe judder and/or bouncing over bumps, amplified by anodized or crud-crusted rims. Certain combinations of fork type and frame geometry can make flutter more of a problem. In my experience, round, thin-gauge, wide-diameter, straight steel fork blades, with a short offset and a fairly steep head angle, are more susceptible to flutter than other types of forks. But I have heard of small-diameter, curved-blade forks fluttering, too. The cheap solution to the problem is to toe in your brake shoes. (See ***brake shoes squeaking or juddering*** in the "Brakes" chapter.) If that and cleaning or sanding your rims don't help, you have to ride home carefully, taking it easy on the bumpy downhills, then buy a different fork.

CHAPTER 6

Wheels and Tires

DESCRIPTION AND DIAGNOSIS: **C** **R** **M** The wheel is the whole round thing you roll on. The tire is the rubber part of the wheel that fits on the metal rim. I know that sounds obvious, but you still hear lots of people say their "tire" is loose, when they mean to say that their wheel is loose.

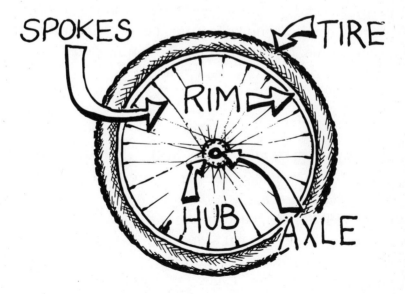

6-1 Wheel Parts

C R M What you have to do most often to wheels is take them off and put them on—to do all kinds of things. (See **Wheel removal** and **Wheel replacement** in the **Flat** portion of this chapter, and read the paragraphs that talk about your kind of bike.)

C R M A flat tire is the most common wheel problem. To fix a flat, go to the **Flat** section. If you don't have a flat, but your **tire is soft,** see the procedure on page 111.

C R M If your wheel is loose or if it's making grindy-crackly noises, see Hub PROBLEMS on page 114. Don't ride with a loose or grindy hub or you may ruin the bearings or even the whole wheel.

C R M If your wheel is bent and wobbly, but it'll still spin around OK, ride it home and either take it off and take it to a pro to be "trued," or see **wheel bent or wobbling** on page 121 for details on how to do the job yourself; make sure you've got lots of time and patience if you haven't trued wheels before; it's all too easy to damage those delicate spokes and rims. If you're stuck out in the sticks with a badly bent wheel and have to get it closer to round so you can ride home, be extra careful about truing that wheel; a long hike is hanging on your efforts.

Tires

PROBLEMS: C R M *Flat.* Bah. You got a flat. Well, don't let it get you down. Follow the procedure below, and you'll soon be on your way. If you do the repair well and keep the tire well inflated, chances are it will be a long time before you get another flat, especially if you are riding a mountain bike; mountain bikes are much less flat-prone than most other bikes. Unless, of course, you live in the thorny Southwest, in which case you might want to put some flat-proofing solution in your tubes.

C R M Flats are due to either slow leaks, quick leaks, or blowouts. No matter what kind of a flat you have, *don't ride the bike on a flat tire! Not even on a soft tire!* The tire, the rim, and your very life are at stake. When you discover you have a flat, just settle down with your patch kit and get to fixing it. If it's a hot day, settle down under a shady tree. If it's raining, find a place out of the rain, so your patch doesn't get wet and lose its stickiness.

C R M First check the valve, if you suspect that it might be the cause. Pump up the tire. Spit on your fingertip and put it lightly over the end of the valve. Tilt your fingertip a wee bit so the only thing between it and the valve end is the spit (on a presta valve, the kind with the tiny metal screw-down cap, you have to use two moist fingers to do this test). If little bubbles come through the spit, your valve stem is leaky. Try pushing the stem in and releasing it a bunch of times (loosen the tiny metal cap first, if you have a presta valve). If that doesn't help and you happen to have a first-aid kit with pointed tweezers in it, you can stick the points of the tweezers down in the valve and tighten the stem in there. If you have one of those two-pronged valve caps you can use that even more easily, but valve caps like that are almost extinct. If you can't fix your leaky valve, you have to go through the wheel and tire removal procedure below, then replace the leaky tube with your spare. If you have no spare tube, you gotta pump the tire up and ride as fast as you can until the air leaks out again; if the valve isn't really shot you can usually ride a half hour or so between pump-ups.

C R M If the valve is OK, but you can hear air hissing out of the tire someplace, find the leak, and if you see the cause (a thorn or piece of glass or whatever), pull the cause out and throw it far from the trail or road. Make a mark on the tire where the hole is. If you don't have a pen or pencil along (even *I* don't carry a pen on mountain bike rides, and

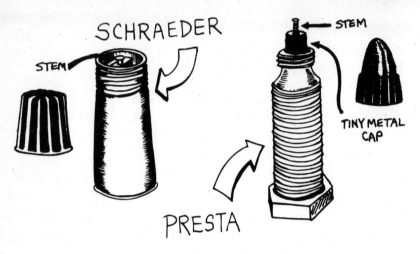

6-2 Two Different Tire Valves

I'm a writer, for crying out loud) you can make a little scratch in the dirt on the side of the tire, or a scratch right on the rubber tread, using a stick or your fingernail.

C R M If you have only one small hole in your tire, and you have a patch kit, you can patch the tube without taking the wheel off the bike. Just lay the bike down on its side and turn the wheel until the part of the tire with the hole is out where you can get at it easily. Then skip down to the section about getting the tire off one side of the rim.

C R M To patch or replace a badly punctured tube, you have to take a bunch of steps. First you hang the bike up, then you remove the wheel, get the tire off, and deal with the punctured tube. Then you put the patched tube or a new tube back in the tire and get the tire back on the rim, and finally you put the wheel back on the bike. The whole song and dance takes some time and patience. If you don't get too harried about it, though, you can usually get going again in about fifteen minutes.

C R M *Wheel removal.* For a start, find something to hang the bike up on, such as a fence post or a low tree limb.

A sturdy bush or a stalwart friend will do. If you have an extra inner tube, you can tie it around the seat tube and sling it over a tree branch. The bike only needs to hang high enough so the wheel with the flat tire is a few inches off the ground.

C R M The next thing to do is look at what's holding the wheel to the bike. There'll be big nuts on the threaded ends of the axle, or a little quick-release lever on the left side of the wheel.

C R M If you have a flat on a front wheel, all you have to do is loosen (c-cl) the nuts or flip the quick-release lever outward, and the wheel will slip out of the front fork. The flat tire should slide right past the brakes, but if it doesn't, mountain bikers, pull the barrel end of the short transverse cable out of its slot on one of the cantilever arms, so the brakes open wide. Road bike people, loosen the brake with the release lever on the mechanism, as shown in Illustration 2-10.

M R If you have a rear-wheel flat (and they're much more common), don't loosen the axle nuts or the quick-release lever just yet. First get the bike in its highest gear. That means getting the chain onto the smallest sprocket on the freewheel. When you're in high gear, loosen the axle nuts or quick-release lever. Then squat behind the bike, put your left hand on the rim of the wheel where it is nearest to you, and with your right hand grab the body of the rear gear changer or "derailleur."

M R Push the wheel forward and down with your left hand as you pull the gear changer and chain back toward you. This action, combined with a gentle jiggling of the wheel, will get the rear sprocket free of the chain. Keep the jiggling to a minimum, so the chain doesn't get tangled up or yanked off the front sprockets as well as the back ones. If the tire hangs up on the cantilever brakes of a mountain bike, pull the barrel end of the short transverse cable out of its slot on one of the cantilever arms, so the cantilevers open up wide. Road bikers can loosen the brakes with the release lever on the mechanism, as shown in Illustration 2-10.

C If you are going to remove a rear wheel from a coaster-brake cruiser, you have to undo the brake arm bracket from the bike frame. Go to the left side of the wheel and look at the thick metal arm that sticks forward along the bike frame from the hub. See the little bracket that holds the end of that arm in place under the frame tube? Unscrew (c-cl) the bolt and nut that hold the bracket tight around the left chain stay (the frame tube). When the bracket is detached from the brake arm, leave the bracket on the chain stay and put the bolt back into its bracket hole and screw (cl) the nut onto it, so those two little parts don't get lost. Then loosen (c-cl) the big axle nuts and slide the rear wheel forward and down to get it out of the frame. Lift the chain off the rear sprocket and you're set to work on the tire.

C R M Once you've got the wheel off the bike (or in a good position to fix a single puncture with a known location), you have to get the tire at least part way off the rim. First push in the little stem tip on the tire valve (on presta valves, loosen the tiny cap before you push the stem tip in) so you get all the remaining air out of the tube. Run your fingers all the way around the tire, squeezing and pinching the beads (edges) together to loosen them if they're stuck to the rim. This will give you an idea of how tough it's going to be to slip the bead of the tire off the rim. It will also loosen the beads as they settle into the "valley" shape of the rim. If the tire is quite loose, all you have to do is grab a section of one bead with both hands and pull away from the center of the wheel, so that the bead of the tire stretches up, as shown in Illustration 6-3.

C R M Lift the stretched-up place over the rim, then work your way around the wheel, spreading the section of bead that has been pulled over the rim. If you are fixing a single known-location puncture with the wheel still on the bike, you only have to pull about one-quarter of the tire bead off the rim; enough to get in there and pull out the section of the tube that has the puncture.

C R M If the tire is a tight high-pressure one and you can't pull a section of the bead over the rim by hand, use your tire irons. Do *NOT* use a screwdriver or any other substitute. Slide the round, spatula-shaped end of your tire iron just barely under one of the beads of the tire. Nudge the sidewall of the tire in with your fingers to make sure the iron doesn't grab on the tube, or go under both beads of the tire and pinch the tube between them. Pinching the tube can easily put a new hole in it, even if you are using proper tire irons. When you have the iron under just one bead of the tire, pry all the way out and down, then hook the handle end on a spoke, as in Illustration 6-3.

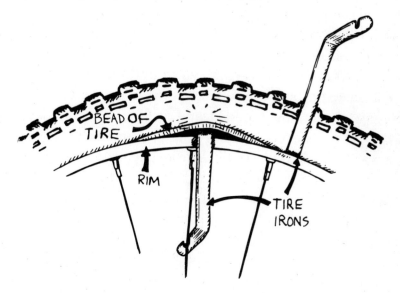

6-3 Using Tire Irons

C R M With a second iron, pry out more of the bead, a couple of inches along the bead from where you made your first pry. If you need to make a third pry and have only two irons, hold the bead outside the rim with your thumb, then pull the second iron out gently, move it a couple inches, and do another pry. Usually two pries will get the tire bead well on its way.

C R M When the bead is on its way (when it doesn't try to jump back onto the rim), take the tire irons out, stick one iron between the popped-out bead and the rim, and peel the rest of the bead out of the rim, just like you'd pare a giant potato peel. Of course, if you have the wheel on the bike still, you single known-location puncture people, you should only peel off the bead about a quarter of the way. Don't take any more off the rim than you have to; that just makes more work putting it back on.

C R M To find the leak, pull as much of tube out of the tire as you can, but leave the valve in place. Pump up the tube until it swells to about two times its normal size. If the thing won't hold any air at all, the leak must be a really bad one, and easy to find. You'll probably have to replace the tube in this case. If the tube does fill up, look for the leak. You may have to move your ear around the tube, listening for it, or even pass the tube close to your eye to feel the leaking air striking the delicate surface of your eyeball. Some pinpoint leaks are hard to spot. Don't wet the tube if you can avoid it; those bubbles from a leak are easy to spot, but the wet tube must be dried *completely* before patching.

C R M When you do find the leak, mark it so you don't forget where it is. If you have a little pen or pencil with you, make arrows or "cross-hairs" pointing at the leak from about one inch away on each side, as shown in Illustration 6-4. If you have no marker, use the sandpaper in your patch kit to "rough up" a 1-inch area of the tube, making sure your leak stays in the exact center of this rough area.

C R M Figure out what kind of hole it is and what made it. Find out *now,* before you forget. There's nothing worse than getting two flats from the same cause. If the hole is a small round one, look for a nail, staple, thorn, or thin shard of glass embedded in the tire casing. If you line the tube up with the tire, it's usually easy to find the culprit. If the hole is a small gash, there will probably be a bigger slash in the casing of the tire. If the tire slash is over ¼-inch long, you have to put a "boot" under it when you put the new or repaired tube back in; otherwise, the new tube will bulge out of the slash like a gum bubble and pop. If you have no boot in your tire kit, you can rig up one from various sturdy, flat objects; I've seen tire boots made out of folded-up swatches of sandpaper, dollar bills, double-layered duct tape, and even a Power Bar (not just the wrapper, the whole THING). If, as you put your boot or whatever inside the tire, you see that the slash in the casing was caused by the brake shoe rubbing on the tire, adjust the brake shoe alignment, as described on page 54; if the brake shoe is rubbing because the spokes of the wheel are all loose and the wheel is slopping all over, tighten the spokes, as described on page 127.

C R M If the hole in the tube is too big to repair and you don't have a spare, here's a trick that may get you home. Cut or tear the tire in half at the hole, then tie the two ends together in a tight knot. Pump up the tube to make sure the knot is airtight. It's hard to stretch this shortened tube back over the rim, and it can be hard to get the tire back on the rim if it's a tight-fit tire, but if you're really stuck with no alternatives, you can usually get the tire to work, and bump-a-lump your way home rather than walking.

C R M If the hole is on the inner side of the tube, look for a sharp spoke end poking through the rim strip. If the rim strip is shot, or missing altogether, you need to rig up a substitute; ½-inch-wide electrician's tape, medical adhesive tape, or even Scotch tape will work in a pinch. If there are two tiny holes on the inner curve of the tube (they're often called "snake bites"), they are probably due to the rim and tire bead pinching the tube when you went over a curb or other hard-edged obstacle; your tire was under-inflated, and, when you went over that bump, the shock of the blow made the tire bead chomp down on the tube.

C R M Remove any puncture-causing debris you find stuck in the tire casing. Run your finger gently around the inside of the casing while you're at it. Might as well root out any sources of further flats before they happen. If the rim is rough (like at its joint) near the point where you have snake bite punctures, use the swatch of sandpaper from your patch kit to smooth out that roughness.

C R M If there's a sharp spoke end sticking up, pull the rim strip away from it, set your screwdriver tip on one side of the spoke end, and whack the screwdriver with a rock or something, as if you were hitting a chisel with a hammer. The idea is to bend the nasty spoke end over, or, if the spoke end is short, to chip it right off. If it's too short to bend over or snap off, file it as smooth as you can with your sandpaper from your patch kit, then put a little wad of rag or paper or a spare tube patch over the thing, so it can't poke through the rim strip and into the tube again. Make a mental note to take the spoke out and replace it with one that's the right length when you get home.

C R M When you have found and removed or filed down the cause of your tube leak, hold your finger over the hole in the tube, pump the thing up again, and listen and look your way around it once more, to make sure there isn't a secondary leak hiding in the woodwork. When you're sure you've found and marked all the leaks and taken care of what caused them, deflate the tube completely.

C R M If you have the wheel off the bike and want to take the tube out to replace or fix it, pull a 6-inch section of the tire bead *that you already took out of the rim* back and all the way over the tube at the valve location. This will leave the tube free to be pulled directly away from the center of the wheel, thus slipping the valve straight out of its hole in the rim. You people with presta valves may have to unscrew a little nut or ring around the threaded stem before you can pull the valve out of the hole in the rim. If you have a spare tube and want to replace your punctured one, just skip the next few paragraphs and go on to the section on how to remount the clincher tube and tire.

C R M If you don't have a spare, or if your spare already has a leak, and you have a small hole, say ⅛ of an inch in diameter or less, you can patch it. Some bike shops refuse to patch any tube with a leak. They just put in new tubes. Haughtily they quote Webster, who states that a patch is a "temporary repair." They pronounce that in their shop, only permanent repairs are done. They have a pretty good point, but if you have only one spare and you get two punctures, and you are miles from the nearest haughty bike shop, you may not give a big damn about the temporary nature of the tire patch. After all, what in the world *isn't* temporary?

C R M Clean and dry the tube around the hole, and rough up the surface with your piece of rough sandpaper if you haven't already done that. Make sure the hole stays at the center of the roughed up area, so you can center a patch of glue around the hole, and/or or stick the patch on with the hole in the center of it, too. The roughing and gluing often hide the hole, so it's best to have those cross-hairs pointing to the hole from outside the scene of action.

C R M If you've never done any patching before, and you have glue-on patches rather than the glueless type, you might want to practice the critical spreading of that thin patch of glue on some other part of the tube where there's no hole. Put the glue on quickly and lightly. Make a smooth, even, thin film of the stuff, larger in area than the size of the patch, but not much larger. Don't squirt out big blobs of glue, either; they don't dry completely. If you hold the lip of the glue container flush against the surface of the tube,

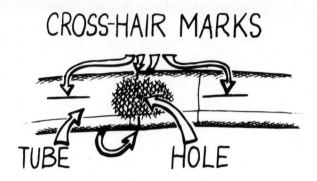

6-4   Roughing up the Tube

then tip up one edge just a bit, you can spread the glue smoothly and evenly into that nice thin film; if necessary, rub the blobs smooth very quickly and lightly with a *clean* fingertip. If you do it right, it'll all look wet and shiny for a few seconds, and then it'll all turn a dull matte texture as it dries. Don't blow on it to make it dry quicker. If you spit or blow damp, misty breath on it, the patch won't stick as well.

C R M If you did a trial glue area, put some dust over it (so it won't stick to the rim and the tire), then go back to the roughed up area around the puncture and do the real thing, to perfection.

C R M Wait a couple of minutes for the glue to dry completely. Make sure no water or dust gets on it. Then take out the patch and eyeball the size to make sure it's going to fit inside the glued area. If you need to apply more glue, do so. Then take the little tinfoil or paper cover off the sticky side of the patch, being careful to keep your fingers off the sticky stuff as much as possible. If there's a thin piece of cellophane on the non-sticky side of the patch, leave it there so you have something to hold and something to push against when the patch is in place. If there isn't any neato cellophane on the patch, or if the cellophane wants to peel off rather than the tinfoil cover, just hold the very edge of

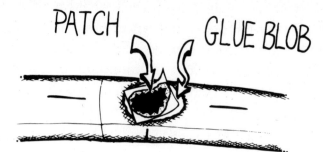

PATCH GLUE BLOB

6-5 Applying the Patch

the patch with one fingernail while you peel the cover off the rest of the sticky side. If you have several punctures and run out of patches, here's a last-ditch trick: Use a piece of duct tape as a patch; just wrap it around the tube, not too tight, and proceed as usual.

C R M Stick the patch, be it glue-on or glueless, in place, making sure it lies down smoothly, without ripples or bumps. Then pinch and knead the patched tube between your fingers, starting at the center of the patch and working out to the edges. Squeeze it as hard as your fingers can, maybe stacking up the first fingers and thumbs of both hands to double your squeezing power. I sit down, put the tube on the hard bone of my knee, and push with stacked thumbs, 'till they hurt. Some people like to use the back end of their pumps or the back sides of the curved end of a plastic tire iron to press down on the patch. Whatever works for you. Just make extra sure it's tight along the little lines or seams on the tube; those seams can make little channels for the air to seep out of if the patch isn't gripping really tight on them.

C R M When you're sure the patch is on there to stay, and stuck well all around the edges, take a little fine dust and poof it around the patch, so any extra glue that's still showing will get a light coating on it. That way it won't stick to the inside of the tire or the wheel rim.

C R M Your patched tube is ready for use immediately. Make one last check before you remount it, though; pump the thing up to about one and a half times its normal size. Run your eye and ear around the tube to make sure it doesn't have any more holes or a leaky stem.

C R M *Remounting the tube and tire.* Start by letting almost all the air out of the tube. If you are putting on a brand new tube, pump a wee bit of air into it so it isn't flat and unmanageable. Find the hole in the rim for the valve and push the free bead of the tire at that point all the way back over the rim until you can see the valve hole. Poke the valve in there, then pull the free bead back over the tube. Working away from the valve in both directions, stuff the tube up into the tire and tuck it into the rim, out of sight and out of your way. If you have to put in a boot to cover a slash in the tire, do it now.

C R M Work the remaining tire bead over the lip of the rim with your thumbs, making sure the tube doesn't get twisted or pinched between the tire bead and the rim. When you get down to the last few inches of the tire bead, it may get tough, especially if you have a tight-fitting tire. First make sure the tube is deflated almost completely and tucked in there out of your way, so you don't pinch it and put a new hole in the thing. Then work your way around the tire, squeezing the two walls together so the two beads settle down into the "valley" shape of the rim as much as possible; this will loosen up that last remaining section of bead. If you can find some "dry lube" like really fine dust or ashes, poof some of it on that last section of the tire bead to help it slide over the rim. Even a dab of spit on the bead may help lubricate it. When you've done all the preparation you can, you have to just roll up your sleeves, focus your energy, and go for it.

C R M Most mountain bike and cruiser tires aren't that hard to mount, but if you have a tough, tight-fitting one, work with both thumbs on one section of the bead, as shown in Illustration 6-6. Don't try to pop the whole thing over the rim at once until you have only a couple of inches to go. It takes a lot of oomph on those thumbs; you can hold one part of the bead in place, like the right hand is doing in the illustration, and roll the rest of the bead into place with the palm or heel of your free hand. Just don't slam the wheel around in your excitement—they bend easily. And *don't* use a screwdriver, or, if you can possibly avoid it, even a tire iron. Anything you stick under the tire at this juncture could reach in there, snatch the tube, and pinch a hole in it.

C R M Just get the bead on a bit at a time. Franz Kafka once wrote, "There is only one human sin—impatience." Not that you can be expected to keep your patience when the tire bites your finger, then jumps off the rim, allowing the tube to flap out at you like a kid sticking out his tongue.

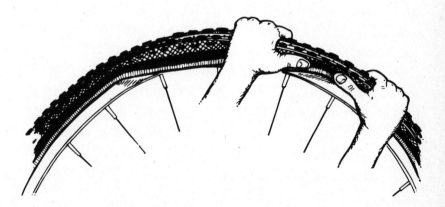

6-6 Pushing the Tire Bead On

Just don't throw the wheel in your anger; they bend, remember.

C R M When you get the bead onto the rim, go back to the valve and push it in and out of the rim a couple of times, wiggling the tire between your fingers as you do so, to make sure the tube isn't pinched between the tire bead and the rim right next to the valve. If it is, the tire will make an annoying thump-thump-thump sound, even on smooth trails or roads. When the tire and tube are seated in the rim as they should be, have a swig of water or Jolt or whatever, relax a bit, then come back and pump the tire up.

C R M If the tire goes flat, do the wet finger test on the valve. If the valve doesn't leak, it must be another hole in the tube. Feel free to yell at it. Call the tire, tube, wheel, and whole bicycle what they are, and start all over. I know exactly how you feel.

C R M If the thing holds air, slap yourself on the back, have another relaxing swig or two, and (if you took the wheel off the bike) go on to the procedure for replacing the wheel on the bike.

C R M *Wheel replacement.* Replacing the repaired wheel is simple if it is a front one. Just make sure the quick-release lever or big axle nuts are loose, then slide the wheel into the forks and tighten (cl) the nuts or push the lever tight (on the left side, of course), checking to see that the rim is centered between the brake shoes as you do the tightening up. Mountain bikers, if you had to undo the brakes to get the tire in or out, push the brake shoes into the rim with one hand and slip the loose end of the transverse cable back into its notch in the cantilever. Roadies, tighten the release lever on the mechanism if you loosened it. You're ready to ride.

M R Replacing a rear wheel is a bit more of a trick. First make sure the axle nuts are loose or the quick-release lever is in its wide-open position. On many bikes, it's even necessary to hold the lever with one hand and the cone thingy on the other side of the wheel with the other, so you can loosen (c-cl) the quick-release to make room for slipping the wheel back into place. If the brakes are tight and it was hard to get the wheel out between them, loosen them. Mountain bikers, you slip the barrel end of the transverse cable out of its little slot on one of the cantilever ends to release the brakes. Roadies, loosen the lever on the mechanism, as shown in Illustration 2-10.

M R Now get in the squat-behind-the-bike position you assumed to pull the wheel out of the frame. Hold the wheel in your left hand, as you did before, and grab the gear changer mechanism with the other. Pull the changer back a bit, so the chain doesn't sag so much. Then jockey the wheel into place in front of the changer, so the upper span of the chain goes over your smallest rear sprocket. Move the wheel up and back into its slots (dropouts) in the frame. If it hangs up on its way into the slots, have a friend fuss with the quick-release or the nuts and washers or the brakes or whatever is causing the hang-up. Just keep one hand on the changer and the other on the wheel so you can move the wheel gently into place.

C To replace a rear wheel on a cruiser, put the chain on the sprocket, slide the wheel into the dropouts, and align it as described in the next paragraph, but also align the brake arm so it can be attached to the little bracket on the left chainstay of the frame. Then tighten the wheel in place with the axle nuts, and use the little bolt and nut to attach the brake arm to its bracket.

C R M Slide your rear wheel as far back as it will go, then line up the tire so it is centered between the chainstays, up forward there near the bottom bracket. If you have vertical dropouts, lining up the wheel correctly is a cinch. Now you can move your right hand from the changer up to the wheel where it's centered, like the guy has done in Illustration 6-7. Keep the wheel exactly centered there while you use your left hand to tighten the quick-release lever on the left side of the wheel. Tighten (cl) both big axle nuts thoroughly with your adjustable wrench if you have axle nuts instead of a quick-release lever.

6-7 Tightening Rear Wheel in Place

M R If you had to loosen the brakes to get the tire in or out, now is the time to tighten them up. Mountain bikers, grab the brake shoes with one hand and squeeze them into the rim, then use the other hand to slip the loose barrel end of the transverse cable back into its slot in the cantilever end. Roadies, tighten the release lever on the mechanism.

C R M When everything is back together, take a little ride around to make sure the brakes, gears, and newly inflated tire all work. If they do, feel free to whoop with delight, and have a good time on the rest of your ride. Keep an eye out for sharp thorns and broken glass, though. . . .

C R M *Tire is soft.* This may be due to a slow leak or the natural seepage of air out of a tube over a long period of time. If you have any suspicion at all that your tire is too soft, do the following foolproof test. You can use a tire gauge instead, but frankly, it won't tell you as accurately what the right tire pressure is *for you.*

C R M To do a nifty *edge test,* find a street curb, rock, or tree root with a relatively sharp edge; something that will serve as a sort of stair-edge. Roll the tire in question up onto the edge, as if the bike is climbing up the "stair." Push down on the bike from above the wheel and watch the tire at the point where it is resting on the "stair" edge as shown in Illustration 6-8. What you are doing here is imitating what happens when you ride over a sharp-edged obstacle.

C R M The edge should flare out the tire, but only a little bit, even if you push down hard and suddenly. The tire should not flare out so much that you feel the "stair" edge clunk against the rim. On the other hand, the tire should not be so hard that there is no flare-out at all when you push down; tires are supposed to absorb the thousands of natural shocks that bikes are heir to, after all. If you do the edge test on a tire and the edge clunks against your rim, pinching the tire and tube, you need to pump up your tire. If you don't pump it up, you'll waste a lot of energy fighting the rolling resistance of the soft tire, and you'll risk getting a snake-bite puncture, as well. Some riders like to vary their tire pressure depending on the terrain—hard for pavement and uphill grinds, softer for off-road and downhilling. That's fine, as long as the tire hardness is within the range that passes the "stair" edge test.

C R M Get a pump that fits well on your type of valve. If you are riding with several other folks who have pumps, find the one that works best on your tire; the better the pump works, the less time the whole group will have to

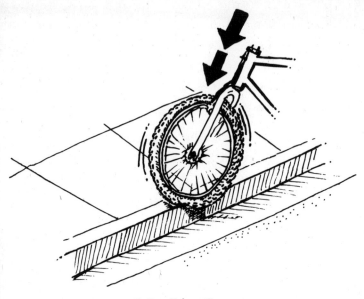

6-8 Edge Test

wait for you to pump up. If you're at home, get a good floor-standing pump with a chuck (the business end) that fits your tire's valve well. If you are inflating tires at a gas station or with a CO_2 powered inflater, *be careful!* Many gas stations have compressors that are made to fill truck tires up to 150 pounds per square inch or more. CO_2 inflators can deliver 125 pounds per square inch or more. That kind of pressure can blow any bike tire clean away! Use the compressed air hose or CO_2 inflator to put little squirts of air into your tire, a couple at a time, then check the bead and do the edge test to make sure you're not over-inflating your tire.

M R If your tire valve is the little skinny presta kind with the tiny screw-down cap at the end, unscrew (c-cl) it and push it down a couple of times to make sure it is loose before you put the pump chuck on the valve and start pumping; air can't get in the tire unless that valve is loose.

C R M Out on the trail or road you will probably be using a frame pump or mini-pump, the kind with the connector right on the end of the pump. You have to make sure you can hold the pump and the bike wheel steady while you pump, so you don't tear the valve off in your efforts to inflate the tire. Lean the bike against a tree, fence post, or boulder, and turn the wheel until the valve is at such a height that you can brace the pump against your left knee while you pump with your right hand. Hold your left hand with your thumb cocked against the rim if you have to for extra stability (left-handers, just reverse all those rights and lefts).

C R M The point of this odd posturing and thumb cocking is to keep the pump from jumping and tipping around in relation to the tire valve. Check to make sure the tire is

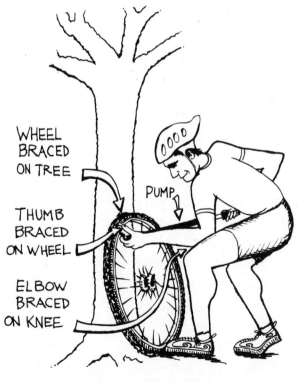

WHEEL BRACED ON TREE

PUMP

THUMB BRACED ON WHEEL

ELBOW BRACED ON KNEE

6-9 Pumping Up

seated well in the rim as you pump it up; the bead should be sunk down into the rim evenly, all the way around. If part of the bead is bulging up and out of the rim, STOP pumping, let all the air out, and work the bead down all around the rim with your fingers to get it all settled into place. Then you can go back to inflating.

C R M Pump, pump, pump, till sweat beads your brow. If you have a small pump and big tires, it will take a fair amount of pumping, but fat tires don't have to be pumped up to a hundred pounds per square inch, so it shouldn't take you long. When the tire feels hard, do a quick edge test again to make sure you are in the permissible range of hardness. Then ride in peace. You have just fixed the root of about half the hardships people ever have with their bikes! If you master the flat, and learn to keep oil on your chain, you are pretty much the master of your mount.

Hubs

DESCRIPTION: C R M The hub is the thing in the center of the wheel that holds the bearings.

PROBLEMS: C R M *Wheel loose or noisy.* Either your wheel feels loose and unsteady under you, or it rubs constantly against the brakes or frame, or the thing makes cracky-grackly noises. Do what you can to fix it, *now*. You may need more tools to do a good overhaul and adjustment at home, but try to get it halfway functional so you can ride home without losing a wheel or destroying the bearings.

C R M If the wheel is noisy, try squirting a little lubricant into the bearings, if they aren't sealed. If they are sealed, or if you don't have any lubricant, just ride home and do a complete overhaul there.

C R M If looseness is the problem, first see if the wheel is loose in the frame. If you wiggle the wheel with your fingers, does the axle slop around in relation to the dropout slot in the frame? If so, tighten (cl) your big axle nuts or your quick-release lever. NOW. Losing a wheel on a downhill is a major mishap.

M **R** If you have a quick-release lever and it isn't holding the wheel firmly even when the lever is pushed all the way in, first try swinging the lever around to the other direction to make sure you are pushing it to its tight position and not to the loose extreme.

M **R** The quick-release lever is loose no matter which way you push it? OK, you have to tighten the unit up. Aim the lever straight out, then grab the little round cone-shaped nut at the other end of the quick-release skewer (over on the other side of the wheel). Hold the round nut still with one hand and turn the lever end of the skewer clockwise a half turn or so. Then push the lever to its tight position and see if it holds the wheel firmly in place. If the lever is still loose, pull it out straight and turn it (cl) again while holding the round nut. It should be pretty hard to lock the lever into its tight position, so the wheel can't jiggle loose.

M **R** There are some super-light quick-release lever units out there that require a last little turn *after* you lock the lever into its tight position. If you have such lever units, turn the lever clockwise to tighten it after locking. This is needed most on rear wheels with non-vertical drop-outs. Personally, I think a lever unit is inadequate if you have to turn it after locking; I'd use it to get home, but then I'd replace it with a slightly heavier but more functional quick-release lever.

C **R** **M** If your wheel still wiggles when the big axle nuts or quick-release lever is tight, your problem is loose cones. It's hard, and sometimes impossible, to get the cones adjusted right without official hub spanners like the ones on page 23. Sometimes you can get by with a Cool Tool and a regular adjustable wrench. If not, you have to limp home and get the proper hub spanners.

C R M Before you fiddle around with the bearing unit, first take a close look at it, and at Illustration 6-10, to identify all the parts. You may see right away that your hub doesn't have locknuts on the outside; if so, you have cartridge bearings, and all you can do is take your loose wheel to a high-tech shop and have them exchange the bearing cartridges. Even if you have regular bearings, you can't see as much of them on your bike as you can in the picture, and at the end of your axle you'll have either a big axle nut or a quick-release lever that partially hides the other stuff. Peer behind and around the obstructions, and wipe off any grime and grease in there so you can see the parts, which appear in this order: first a big nut or quick-release lever, then the drop-out of the frame, then a thin locknut, then a washer, and then a cylindrical cone, which disappears into the hub but has two slots that are visible at its outside edge—those slots are for a thin spanner.

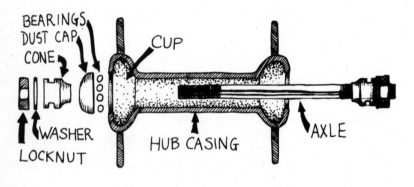

6-10   Hub, Exploded View

C R M Know what the parts on your hub are now? Great. The procedure for adjusting the cones will be different, depending on whether you have quick-release levers or not, and depending on whether it's a front or rear wheel you're working on. Find the paragraph below that applies to you and go for it.

C R M If you have a front wheel with big axle nuts, tighten (cl) one of them so the wheel will stay in place, and loosen (c-cl) the other. Then, on the side of the wheel with the loose axle nut, reach behind the drop-out with a thin-jawed wrench, such as a hub spanner or the adjustable wrench on a Cool Tool. Get the jaws of the tool onto the slots of the cone and turn it clockwise until it is snug on the bearings. If the locknut is not tight against the cone and washer, you can even snug the cone in with your fingers. Back the cone off a quarter turn or less, then tighten (cl) the locknut against the cone and tighten (cl) the big axle nut on that end of the axle, too. See if the wheel can spin smoothly. If the bearings are too tight, you have to loosen (c-cl) all the nuts and stuff outside the cone, then loosen the cone (c-cl) a bit, then tighten (cl) everything back up again.

M R If you have a front wheel with a quick-release lever, pull the lever out and take the wheel off the bike, then see if either cone-and-locknut set is still tight against itself, so the parts can't be turned around the axle. Put a regular adjustable wrench on the locknut of the tight set. Adjust the wrench carefully so it fits tight on the flats of the locknut (some locknuts have slots, so you have to use a thin-jawed wrench instead). Tighten (cl) the cone on the other side of the hub with your fingers, or a thin-jawed wrench such as a hub spanner or the adjustable wrench on a Cool Tool. Just snug the cone up on the bearings, then back it off a quarter turn or less. Tighten (cl) the locknut against the washer and cone, using your thin-jawed wrench, holding the other end of the axle still with a regular adjustable wrench. Then take the regular adjustable wrench off that far locknut, and while you hold the cone still with the thin-jawed wrench, tighten (cl) the nearby locknut against it with the adjustable wrench. Then take all wrenches off the bearing parts, grab the locknuts and the ends of the axle with your fingers, and give the wheel a spin. If it rolls easily without slopping around on the bearings too much, put the wheel back on the bike and get riding. If the bearings are too tight (the spinning wheel will tug at your fingers holding the axle), you have to loosen (c-cl) the locknut you just tightened, loosen (c-cl) the cone a bit more, then tighten (cl) the lock- nut again.

C R M If you have a rear wheel with big axle nuts, tighten (cl) the axle nut on the right side of the bike. Next loosen (c-cl) the big axle nut on the left side, where there aren't any sprockets and gear changers in your way. Then use a thin-jawed wrench such as a hub spanner or the adjustable wrench on a Cool Tool to first loosen (c-cl) the left-side locknut, then snug (cl) the cone in against the bear- ings. Back the cone off a quarter turn or less, then tighten (cl) the locknut against the cone and tighten the axle nut so the whole wheel is held firmly in place again. Give the wheel a spin. If it rolls OK without a lot of slop, ride on it. If the bearings are tight now, loosen (c-cl) the nuts on the left end of the axle again, then loosen (c-cl) the cone a bit more, then tighten (cl) those other nuts again.

M R If you have a quick-release rear wheel, put the bike in its highest gear, so the chain is on the smallest sprocket, then take the wheel off the bike. See page 96 if you want some hints on this. When you have the wheel off, put your adjustable wrench on the locknut that is the only part of the bearing unit showing on the right side of the hub, just vis- ible in the middle of all the sprockets. Adjust the wrench carefully so it fits tight on the flats of the locknut (some locknuts have slots, so you have to use a thin-jawed wrench or hub spanner instead). Then reach around to the other side of the hub and use a thin-jawed wrench such as a hub spanner or the adjustable wrench on a Cool Tool to tighten (cl) the left cone until it is snug against the bearings. Back it off (c-cl) a quarter turn or so, then tighten (cl) the locknut against the washer and cone. Then take the adjustable wrench off the locknut on the sprocket side of the wheel and use it to tighten (cl) the other locknut firmly against the washer and the cone you adjusted, holding that cone still with your thin-jawed wrench. After doing this final tighten-up, take all wrenches off the bearing parts, grab the lock-nuts and the ends of the axle with your fingers, and give the wheel a spin. If it rolls easily without slopping around on the bearings, put the wheel back on the bike and ride. If the bearings are too tight (the spinning wheel will tug at your fingers holding the axle), you have to loosen (c-cl) the lock-nut, loosen (c-cl) the cone a bit more, then tighten (cl) the locknut again. When you re-mount the adjusted wheel, make sure the quick-release lever is holding it very firmly in place. If it isn't, see page 115 for the method to tighten up the quick-release mechanism.

[C] Look at the left side of any cruiser hub (except on a coaster brake rear wheel; it has brake stuff on the left side, so you gotta look at the *right* side, as explained on the next page). Starting at the left end of any axle, you should have first a big nut, then the drop-outs (the slot in the frame that holds the wheel), then a thin locknut, then a washer, then the cylindrical cone that disappears into the hub and has two slots at its outside edge for a thin spanner. Your wheel may have no thin locknut. In that case, the big axle nut acts as a locknut. Think of it as such in this whole section, and do your adjustment with the wheel *on* the bike.

[C] You *must* have a spanner that fits into the slots in the cones to work on your hub. Campagnolo makes a good set, if you can get it. But don't mess with your hub unless you have a thin spanner to fit it.

[C] Your hub may have a slotted cone on only one end of the axle. If so, don't mess with the end that has no slot in its cone (the slotted cone should be on the left side, but this isn't always the case). Loosen (c-cl) only the left big axle nut. Tightening the cones should be done with the wheel held in place by the right big axle nut.

C Get your thin spanner in the slots on the left cone, tighten (cl) the cone up on the bearings, and back it off (c-cl) about a half turn, until the wheel spins easily. Then tighten (cl) the left thin locknut (or big axle nut) down against the washer and cone. This may tighten up the cone on the bearings. If it does, use two spanners, one backing the left cone (c-cl) and one tightening (cl) the left thin locknut. When you have the cone and thin locknut set so that the wheel spins smoothly but doesn't wiggle from side to side, tighten (cl) the big nut. Spin the wheel, then ride the bike, to make sure the bearing is smooth. If it isn't, or if it's making lots of weird crackly grinding noises, see the hub overhaul procedure, below.

C To adjust the bearings on the rear wheel of a bike with coaster brakes, tighten (cl) the LEFT axle nut, then you can adjust the cone on the RIGHT side of the wheel, over there where the sprocket is. Loosen (c-cl) the right axle nut, loosen (c-cl) the big locknut, tighten (cl) the cone down on the bearings with a cone wrench (it usually requires a special big cone wrench) and then back it off about a quarter turn. Then tighten (cl) both the big locknut and the big axle nut. Make sure the wheel spins freely, but without sloppy side-to-side play; a coaster brake hub can self-destruct if the bearings are either too loose or too tight.

C R M *Hub overhaul*. If you have adjusted a wheel hub and it still is making lots of nasty noises, you need to overhaul the thing. You can do this on most bikes, but there are exceptions. If the wheel is a rear one from a 3-speed bike, take it to a good shop for overhaul—special tools and know-how are needed. If it is a coaster-brake cruiser, see page 58 for the overhaul procedure. To overhaul a road- or mountain-bike hub, take the wheel off of the bike, as in the adjustment procedure, above. Remove the quick-release skewer if there is one (turn the cone-shaped end c-cl). Then loosen (c-cl) the locknut on one side of the hub, take it and the washer off, then spin (c-cl) the cone off, take the axle and bearings out of the wheel, and clean all of the parts. If you find rough places on any of the ball bearings or on either of the cones, replace them (if the races in the hub are rough, alas, you have to replace the whole wheel). Grease all your clean or new hub parts. Put the hub back together the way it came apart, and adjust the bearings as described above.

Spokes and Rims

DESCRIPTION: **C** **R** **M** The rim is the thin aluminum (or steel) hoop that your tire fits on. Spokes are the lacy wires that keep the rim round. They do it by pulling evenly, all the way around the wheel. At the rim end of each spoke there is a nipple that can be turned tighter or looser to increase or decrease the tension on the spoke so it pulls evenly with its fellow spokes. The rim and spokes of a wheel weigh about two pounds. They withstand forces that boggle the imagination every time you fly over a jump or slam into a large rock. Needless to say, spokes can break and rims can bend. It is miraculous that they don't get broken and bent more often.

PROBLEMS: **C** **R** **M** *Wheel bent or wobbling.* You hit a bad bump, or went into a rut or something, and one of your wheels is no longer round. It's no fun to ride on a bent wheel, but if you can get home on it, do so. Truing a wheel properly is a high art. If you want to do it yourself, practice the art in peaceful, unpressured surroundings, using the *truing a minor wobble* procedure on page 127 to help you. Or, take the job to a pro.

C R M If, however, you are out on the trail or road and have a wheel that's so bent it won't get you home, here are some things you can try to do in order to get it rolling.

C R M If the wheel is hitting on the brakes, but not the frame, loosen the brakes with the adjusting sleeve, as shown in Illustration 2-6. This will mean you have to ride home with only one good brake, so ride cautiously.

C R M If the rim is sprung out of round, so the wheel looks like a potato chip (some people say it's pretzeled, others say tacoed) and the tire slams from one side to the other if you try to spin the wheel, hitting the brakes and all the frame stays, you've got to resort to drastic methods if you're going to be able to ride home at all.

C R M First look at the wheel from above it to get an idea of just how bad the bends are and how many there are. If the whole wheel has been reduced to a cupped-hand shape, as shown in Illustration 6-11, you have a classic example of a sprung wheel. If only one short section of the wheel is bent out to one side from the center, with perhaps two small sections bent the other way, one on either side of the main bend, you have a one-point-impact bend. It's usually easier to fix up enough to ride on. Skip the sprung wheel melodrama below, and go on to the single-bend straightening procedure, six paragraphs down.

C R M A sprung wheel may well be hopeless. But true boonie bikers never give up hope until they are forced to. So here's a last-ditch wheel-saving trick you can try. You've got nothing to lose, as long as you don't get so rough you crack the wheel hub.

C R M Take the wheel off the bike (see page 96 if you need advice on this) and let a little air out of the tire, if it is pumped up really hard. (60 pounds of pressure or more.) Then find a tree or post or vertical boulder that has a root or small rock sticking out about a foot from the base. What you want are two solid objects to brace the opposing sections of the rim against, as shown in Illustration 6-11. If either bracing point is a rock, pad it with some cloth or a spare tire or something, so you don't munch the rim even worse than you have already. You can even use a short hunk of log braced against a tree. Be creative. Set things up so you have the wheel resting against something solid at the top and the bottom.

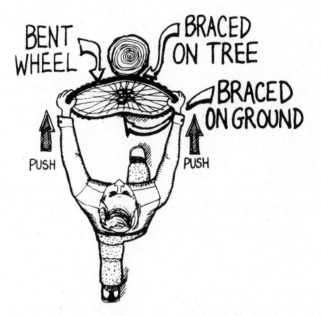

6-11   Last-Ditch Wheel Straightening

C R M Now, the points of the rim that should be braced are the ones that are bent farthest *away* from you; the points are bent toward the tree or rock, in other words. If the top and bottom of the wheel are bent toward you, just rotate the wheel 90 degrees so the bends are going the right way.

C R M Put the heels of your hands on the parts of the rim that are bent closest to you. If these points are near the bottom bracing point, rotate the wheel a half turn, so they are nearer to the *top* of the wheel. When your hands are placed correctly, give a gentle shove, leaning the weight of your body into it. Push gently a couple of times to get the feel of things, then harder once—a good, sharp shove. This should bend the wheel considerably if you really put your body into the shove. Sometimes the wheel pops back into a shape that's almost round. If it goes round, then pops back into a potato-chip shape, try again, just a wee bit harder, but not so hard that you spring it the other way. Sometimes, especially with narrow rims, the thing will suddenly spring into a shape that's surprisingly close to straight. If this happens, don't argue with success.

C R M Pump up the tire a bit if it's really soft, but keep the pressure on the low side. Then wrap any broken spokes around their neighbors to keep them out of trouble, and ride home with a song in your heart. When you get home, you can try to do a real truing job, as described on page 127, or better yet, replace the rim, or just take the wheel to a pro.

C R M If one of the bends comes out of the wheel when you shove on it, but you still have a single bend left over, or a bend and a couple of secondary bends going the other way, fix them according to the method that follows.

C R M If you have a single bend from a run-in with a big rock, or one big bend with a couple little ones going the other way on either side, first see if you can get the wheel somewhere nearer to straight by using a variation on the last-ditch effort shown in Illustration 6-11. Turn the wheel so the big bend is at the top of the wheel, *bowing away from you*. If there are mini-bends, they will now be at either side of the big bend, and curving toward you.

C R M Let a little air out of the tire if it is pumped up really hard, then lean the big bend against your upper bracing object. Make sure the bracing object is padded if it's a rock, then put the heels of your hands on either side of the big bend (right on the secondary bends, if the wheel has them) and give a short, sharp shove. Don't heave your whole body into the shove unless you weigh less than 120 pounds. The idea is to shove with your arms until you feel the metal of the rim give just a bit. The thing may go almost straight the first time you shove, or it may take three or four little shoves. Don't push too hard in any case; you don't want to bend the thing the other way, or spring the whole wheel into a potato chip.

C R M When the wheel is roughly round, so it can at least spin without hitting the frame, you can loosen your brakes and ride it home, then do a good truing job on it, or take it to a pro.

C R M If you have a spoke wrench, lots of time and patience, and a gentle touch with things mechanical, you can try to get a bent rim pretty close to true by adjusting the spokes, so you can leave your brakes tight and go on riding. But truing a wheel out in the boonies only makes sense if you have a *long* way to ride. If you have any broken spokes, you usually can't get the wheel close to true without some spare spokes.

C R M Before you start wildly twiddling with the spokes, first make sure the tire isn't rock hard (let some air out if it is), then spin the wheel and look closely at the rim as it goes past the brake shoes. Look for "blips" as well as wobbles. A blip is a little outward flare or bump in the rim, caused by hitting a sharp object like the edge of a rock or a curb. Your brakes will grab on this blip, causing skids and tire wear. If you find a blip, fix it first, then straighten the bend with the spokes.

C R M To *fix a blip*, you need a special tool—a vise-grip wrench—and a keen sense of how to use that tool. Don't use any other tool. If you are on the trail or road, you'll probably have to skip the blip, fix your wobbles as much as possible, and limp home.

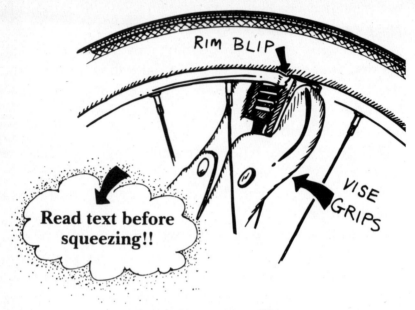

6-12   Squeezing a Blip

C R M When you have a vise-grip, adjust the jaws (using the knob at the end of one handle) so that they are wide enough to fit around the width of the rim when the handles of the vise-grip are *clamped shut.* Stick the vise-grip between the spokes of the wheel at the point where you have the blip (see Illustration 6-12). Center the blip in the jaws of the vise-grip and adjust the jaws so that they will *just barely* hold onto the blip when the handles of the tool are locked closed. Now stop. You have, at your fingertips, potential for the total destruction of the roundness of your rim. If the rim is a high-tech lightweight one, it may have very thin walls; you might want to take it to a shop and see if they can fix it or replace it. But if you are willing to proceed, look closely at what you are about to do. Are there blips on both sides of the rim? The vise-grip will squeeze equally from both sides.

C R M If you have a larger blip on one side than on the other, squeeze both sides of the rim until the little-blip side is flat. Then take a small, thin piece of wood, like a popsicle stick, and put it along the flattened side of the rim. Adjust the jaws of the vise-grip so that they accommodate the popsicle stick when the handles are snapped all the way closed. Then release the little trip-lever that is on one of the vise-grip handles, and, as you keep the jaws barely gripping the rim with one hand, tighten (cl) the adjusting knob of the vise-grip so the jaws move closer to the rim. Turn the knob about a half turn and squeeze the handles together. Watch the rim, looking at it from a tangent. If the blip is still sticking out, tighten the vise-grip adjusting knob again, a half turn or less, and squeeze slowly. Watch as you squeeze. Stop squeezing if you're going to go too far before the vise-grip locks. *Keep in mind that you can't unsqueeze the rim!*

C R M When the blip has been squeezed in even with the rest of the rim, don't be surprised if there are two small dents, one on either side of where the blip was. They won't hurt your braking like the blip. Spin the wheel and check for a wobble. A wobble often comes along with a blip.

C R M To ***true a minor wobble,*** first let some air out of the tire, if you haven't already. Next tighten the brakes, if the wobble isn't already hitting one brake shoe or the other. If you have a brake adjusting sleeve (see Illustration 2-6), use it. If you don't have one, find a chip of wood or a little stick, apply the brakes, then jam the wood thingie into the gap that opens between the brake hand lever and the brake handle post (see Illustrations 2-2, 2-3, and 2-4) so the brake shoes are held in close where they'll touch the rim at the wobble.

C R M Now, to get the wheel closer to straight, you want to move the section of the rim that's hitting the brake shoe away from it. This is done by alternately tightening and loosening a bunch of spokes, using a spoke wrench. For instance, to move the rim to the *left, tighten* (cl) the nipples of the spokes that go to the *left* side of the hub and *loosen* (c-cl) the nipples of the spokes that go to the *right* side of the hub, as shown in Illustration 6-13.

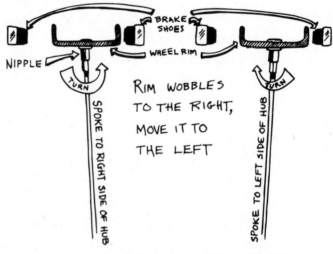

6-13 Straightening a Minor Wobble

C R M As you tighten and loosen spoke nipples, keep a couple of things in mind. The ideal wheel has exactly the same amount of tension on every spoke. So, in your adjusting, don't leave any spoke completely loose, and don't tighten just one spoke in order to do all the work of moving the rim over. Think of a wobble as the result of a group of six or eight maladjusted spokes—not just one errant individual, but a misfit minority.

C R M To move the rim laterally, you want to adjust the whole group of six or eight nipples. If any of the spokes in the group you are working on is obviously much too tight or much too loose, you have to try to bring it into the same range of tightness as the other spokes in the group.

C R M Try to pick up the "feel" of the median tension of all the spokes. One way to get that feel is to go around the whole wheel, tightening and loosening every spoke about a tenth of a turn. It takes a while, but it's a good warm-up exercise, especially if you aren't a hotshot wheelmaker. You might find, right away, that all or most of the nipples are rusty and frozen tight to the spokes, so they won't turn at all. If your wheel has a lot of frozen nipples (a very uncomfortable condition, I'm sure), use the last-ditch straightening method on page 122 and try to get the wheel round enough to carry you home, then take it to a pro. If you try to fix it with your spoke wrench out on the trail or road, you'll probably just break a bunch of spokes or strip the flats off the nipples.

C R M You might find that all or most of your spoke nipples are loose. Most likely, the factory or shop that put your bike together didn't tighten up the spokes enough, so the whole thing is coming apart on you. This is a really serious problem. It can lead to brake shoes jamming in the spokes or wearing holes in the tire sidewalls. As if that isn't bad enough, you can make the wheel much *worse* if you don't do the tightening carefully—so the increasing tension stays even all around the wheel.

C R M The best solution to general spoke looseness is to just go around the wheel tightening every spoke a half turn at a time with your bare fingers (if you come across a couple of really loose spokes, tighten each one up until it is close to finger-tight like the others). When they're all finger-tight, start at the tire valve and make one more trip around the rim, turning each spoke EXACTLY ONE-HALF TURN with your spoke wrench. If the wheel is still really loose and wobbly, take another trip around the rim giving each spoke a half turn. But DON'T tighten the spokes more than a half turn at each trip around the rim! When the whole wheel seems pretty tight (each nipple takes a little oomph to tighten) go on with this straightening procedure and try to get the wheel round enough to get you home. Don't expect anything near perfection; hops, wobbles, and general egg-shapeness are likely, unless you have a natural knack for the art. Just get the wheel round enough so the rim and the tire sidewalls miss the brake shoes; then make a mental note to take the wheel to a first-rate bike shop and have a wheel expert re-true it, as soon as possible.

C R M Even if the spoke nipples turn OK and aren't all loose, you will find variations in the tension of the spokes. This is especially true of rear wheels. The rear wheels of most multispeed bikes are flattened or "dished" to compensate for the sprockets being on one side. Look down on your rear wheel from above and you'll see how the spokes go out farther on the left than they do on the right. If the wheel is made just right, this won't mean that those right spokes are too tight, but in far too many cases, the right spokes have been cinched in extra tight to dish the wheel.

C R M So, when you work on a rear wheel, you'll often find that half the spokes are much tighter than the others, and you have to accept their tightness when fixing a wobble. Even on a front wheel, you may find some spokes have been over-tightened to make up for an imperfection in the rim or something.

C R M The whole point is, try for a *close-to-round* wheel; don't try to make the wheel absolutely perfect. Work to create *some* lateral movement of the bent portion of the rim, to straighten it enough so you can use it to get home. And do this without putting too much or too little tension on any one spoke. If you are at home and have the time and patience, you can work toward a very-close-to-perfect wheel, but still, it may wind up with some slight flaws.

C R M Twiddle the spokes at your wobble a bit at a time, loosening the ones to the same side of the hub as the wobble and tightening the spokes to the opposite side of the hub from the wobble, as in Illustration 6-13. Adjust the whole group of six or eight spokes, then check to see how much you've improved the wobble. Be careful you don't generate secondary wobbles on the ends of your original wobble. Tighten and loosen the spokes more in the middle of the wobble and do less tension adjustment near the ends of the wobble.

C R M If you get the wobble close enough to straight so the wheel will spin freely between the brake shoes, don't try to take things any further. Ride home and do a primo job when you have more time, or take the wheel to a pro if you aren't satisfied with your slightly wobbly wheel. I don't mind having a little wobble or two in my rear wheel, because I never look back there; I'm pickier about front wheel wobbles because I have to stare at the front wheel as I'm grinding up those long grades.

C R M If you begin to have trouble with your one big wobble turning into several frustrating small ones, and you begin to lose patience, *quit now*. Go get a drink of water, have a Fig Newton, look at the scenery for a minute. Whatever it takes to calm down. If you don't, those spokes can start playing coyote tricks on you. Wobbles appear magically where moments before there was only straightness. One big gentle wobble turns into three sharp little ones; a totally new wobble appears on the other side of the wheel. That sort of thing. It can get like the scene in *Fantasia* with Mickey Mouse and the multiplying brooms.

C R M With some experience, you will learn the elusive "feel" of spoke tension that controls all those secondary wobbles. But if you are new to the game, and stuck out in the country somewhere, close-to-round is close enough.

C R M If you have a pump or tire inflater, before you pump your tire up on your usably round wheel, check for spoke ends sticking up through the rim. Let all of the air out of your tire. Put a finger under the tire and run it around the rim strip. If there are spoke ends sticking up through the rim strip, or even poking big bumps up in the strip, take the wheel off the bike and take the tire off the wheel so you can take care of those sharp spoke ends, as explained in the **_Flat tire_** procedure on page 102.

C **R** **M** **_Broken spokes._** These are most common for heavy riders who do not have heavy-duty rear wheels. If you bust a single spoke on a short ride, and the wheel doesn't have too bad a wobble because of it, or if you can use the method described in the previous section to get the wobble tolerably straight, just wrap the broken spoke around one of its neighbors to keep it from snagging on things and making weird noises, then ride home. Once home, you can take a whole spoke off the wheel and get a correct replacement for the broken one from a shop, or have the wheel fixed and trued by a pro. You can fix the thing yourself, but frankly, if you are heavy (say, over 200 pounds) and your wheel is not a heavy-duty one, it's gonna be hard for you to true your wheel well enough to prevent further spoke breakage.

C **R** **M** If you break more than one spoke, and you are out in the middle of nowhere, and you have a long way to go to get to any bike shop with a hotshot wheelsmith, and if you have some spare spokes, a spoke wrench, and (for rear-wheel work) a freewheel remover or chain whips (all these things are described in the _Tools_ section of Chapter 1), you can replace your broken spokes by yourself. The job can be a real pain, but you should do it to prevent further spoke breakage and increasingly bad wheel wobbles. A really bad wheel wobble can ruin your brakes and even weaken the frame if the tire rubs badly.

C **R** **M** First take the wheel off the bike and take the tire off the rim, as described on pages 96–99. Peel back the rim strip so you can see the spoke nipples of the broken spokes. Take the ends of the broken spokes out of the hub and the rim. If you are working on a rear wheel, chances are the broken spokes are on the side of the hub that's blocked by the cluster of sprockets on your freewheel or cassette. Turn to page 180 to see how to remove your freewheel or cassette, and when you have taken if off the wheel, come back here to continue with the spoke replacement procedure.

C R M When you have removed a broken spoke and its nipple from the wheel, take a new spoke in hand and line it up next to one that's already on the wheel to make sure it's the right length. If the head of the spoke is even with the hole in the hub, the other end of it (the one with the threads) should just reach the rim.

C R M Push the new spoke into the hub so it goes through the hole the same way the old one did. The spokes that go through the hub-holes on either side should be the other way around. For instance, if the head of your spoke winds up on the outside of the hub flange, the two adjacent spokes should have their heads on the inside of the flange. Pull the new spoke through the maze of others, and get it so it's pointing straight out at the rim, without touching any of those other spokes. You may have to curve the spoke a little to get it woven through there, but that's OK as long as you don't put a sharp bend in it. A gently curved spoke will straighten out as you tighten it up.

C R M When you have pulled the spoke all the way through, so its head is seated against the hub flange, it will not be pointing at the hole for it. To get it aimed at its proper hole, first look at the two spokes whose heads are on either side of the new one in the hub flange. These spokes will both run out to the rim in the same direction, either forward or back. The spokes must alternate, so if the two spokes on the sides of your new one go forward, make yours go back, or vice versa. Move your spoke end through its brothers, like a dancer weaving through a Virginia reel, until it points at the hole in the rim. It should be able to barely stick into that hole, or at least come quite close to sticking into it.

C R M Now check to see if the other spokes in the wheel are "laced." On almost all bikes, the spokes cross each other several times on the way out to the rim. On laced wheels (which most quality production bikes have), the spokes touch at the point where they cross nearest to the rim. This is for lateral stability. If your wheel is laced, make sure you weave the new spoke through the old ones to match the lacing of the other spokes around the wheel. For instance, if all forward-going spokes lace *over* all backward-going spokes, lace a new forward-going spoke so it goes *over* the backward going spoke that it crosses as it nears the rim.

C R M Insert the nipple through the hole for your new, correctly laced spoke. Spin the nipple onto the spoke and tighten it with your fingers at first. Put the tire back on the rim and your wheel back on the bike. Then true the wheel, as explained on page 127, making sure the new spoke gets into the same range of tightness as the ones around it. That way the wheel won't be overstressed any more, and if you ride carefully, you probably won't break any more spokes on your way home.

C R M Do a first-rate truing job when you get home, or have a pro do it. If you are a heavy or hard-driving rider and do mountain biking or touring, get special heavy-duty wheels made for you; mountain biking in particular asks a lot of your spoked wheels. Make sure they are in the best possible shape for future rides.

CHAPTER 7

Seat or Saddle and Seat Post

DESCRIPTION: **C** **R** **M** The seat is the leather or plastic thing you sit on. It is attached by a strong wire frame and a bracket or clamp to a seat post. The post is held by a binder bolt at the top end of the seat tube of the bike frame, or it is clamped there by a quick-release lever. (See Illustration 7-2.) Sizes, shapes, hardnesses, and durabilities of different seats vary widely. If you plan to ride long distances, you should get a quality nylon, leather-covered nylon, or top-grade butt leather seat.

C **R** **M** You *can* get a comfortable seat if you shop around. The ones with carefully placed soft spots or cutout spaces, like the Terry seats, are especially good for people with tender points. Terry seats, first designed *by* women, *for*

135

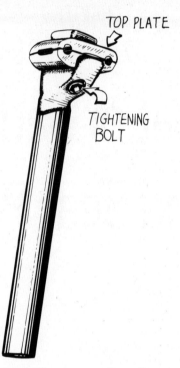

TOP PLATE

TIGHTENING
BOLT

7-1 Clamp-top Seat Post

women, are now made for men, kids of both genders, and
even saddle-sore old geezers! Kudos to you, Terry!

C R M Seat brackets, which fit on the top end of plain
seat posts, are standardized at ⅞ inch. The kind of seat post
that has a clamp built onto the top has standardized slots for
the seat frame rails. But the o.d.'s (outside diameters) of seat
posts where they fit into the seat tube of the bike frame are
anything but standardized. They vary from about ⅞ inch to
1⅛ inch. They are often calibrated on a metric scale.

C R M The clamp-top seat posts are often adjustable to a
much finer degree than the standard seat brackets. If you
have one of these fancy units, all you need is the right size
Allen wrench to adjust the seat's position. And once you adjust the seat and tighten it into place, it will stay there; the
bracket seat mounts tend to strip out and come loose.

Ⓜ A note for those of you who have mountain bikes with quick-release binder bolts holding your seat post in the frame: thieves tend to steal seats that are held in by quick-release binder bolts. This is a *most* inconvenient drawback for a convenience item. One solution is to get a special custom binder bolt that works just like a quick-release, but does not have a lever. Instead, it has a hole in the end for an Allen wrench. You just stick the Allen wrench in there and use it like a lever. Unless a bike thief has this Allen wrench (most casual bike thieves won't), your seat is secure.

PROBLEMS: Ⓜ Ⓡ *Seat tips up and down.* If the seat is on a clamp-top seat post, get an Allen key that fits the tightening bolt or bolts on the clamp that is at the top of the post. Loosen (c-cl) the bolt or bolts first, so you can adjust the seat to the angle you want (it should be near level). Then tighten (cl) the bolt or bolts thoroughly. As you tighten, shift the seat slightly every once in a while to make sure it is settling into the right grooves in the mounting clamp.

Ⓒ If you have an old-fashioned seat on a cruiser with a bracket holding the seat, get a box-end, open-end, or crescent wrench that fits the tightening nuts exactly, and tighten them up. Tighten them evenly, doing a few turns on one, then a few on the other, and as you tighten, shift the seat slightly every once in a while to make sure that the bracket is sitting firmly in the position you want. If you have lots of trouble with your seat bracket coming loose, I recommend you buy a new seat post, the kind with the clamp built onto the top end.

Ⓒ Ⓡ Ⓜ If your *seat swivels from side to side*, or the whole post slides down into the frame tube so the seat is too low, you have to tighten the quick-release or binderbolt that holds the seat post in the bike frame. First loosen the quick-release lever or loosen (c-cl) the binder bolt, then move the seat to the right height for you. I'm not going to tell you what that height should be, but generally riders like the seat set at such a level that when they sit on it, they can put the pedal at the bottom of its stroke, stretch their leg out straight, and rest their heel flat on the pedal. Much higher, and you have to rock your fanny to pedal; much lower and your knees have to bend too much at the top of each pedal stroke. Measure pedal length with *your* seater centered on the bike seat so that as you pedal along the trail or road *your* seater doesn't rock from side to side on the bike seat, thus creating undo friction and saddle sores.

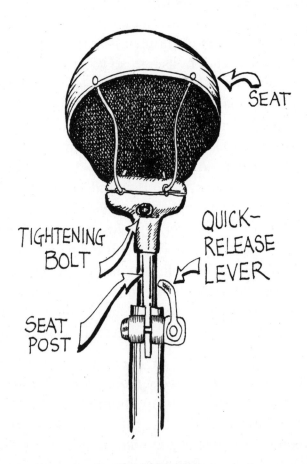

7-2 The Seat

C R M When you get the seat where you want it, look down on the seat from above and make sure it is pointing straight ahead, so the tip of it is lined up with the center of the top tube of the bike, then tighten (cl) the binder bolt, or hold the lever end of the quick-release unit and tighten (cl) the cone end a half turn or so, then clamp the lever down all the way. Make sure the seat post is held firmly in place. Some seat-post binders require tightening one or more Allen bolts. Others have hard-to-reach hex-bolt heads. Get the tool that fits on your setup, be patient, and make sure you get that binder tight, one way or the other.

C R M If no amount of patient tightening on the binder bolt will tighten the frame tube enough to hold the seat post still, you must have a post that's too small for your frame tube. Not to worry. If you can find an aluminum can, you can fix up your loose seat post in a jiffy. Just cut a rectangular piece of aluminum out of the side of the can, about 1 inch by 2½ inches in size. Use a sharp knife to do the cutting, and cut the edges as clean as possible, smoothing off any burrs or bumps along the edges by wrapping the piece of aluminum around your seat post, then rubbing the edges flat with the edge of the handle of your knife or something, then sanding the leftover burrs off with the little swatch of sandpaper from your tire patch kit.

C R M The resultant curved, smooth-edged swatch of aluminum can be used as a "shim" to make your seat post wider. Just loosen the binder bolt or quick release all the way, pull out the seat post, then wrap the shim around the seat post and slide the whole business down into the frame. If the frame is now too tight, use a big screwdriver to pry the top of the frame tube a bit wider apart. Slide the seat post and shim in carefully, so the shim doesn't get mashed out of shape. Adjust the seat height and get the seat pointing straight ahead, then tighten (cl) the binder bolt or the quick-release lever.

C R M If, by some chance, you have a post that is too big for your frame tube, don't force it into the tube. It will stretch and weaken the frame at that point. Get a post that fits, or get one that's too small and shim it.

C R M **Sore seater**. Arrgh. This is a nasty problem, especially on a long ride. What to do? The short, cruel answer is "get tough!" You should have taken a bunch of short rides to get toughened up before you took off on a long ride. But there are some things you can do to limit the agony if you are out on a long ride and have to get home somehow.

C R M First off, make sure your pants are clean and as dry as possible where you sit, and that they don't get bunched up under there. Tight cycling shorts with a clean, soft liner in the crotch are best. If you don't have these, just do the best you can to keep your pants clean and smooth underneath you. Ever wonder why cowpokes like often-washed, shrink-to-fit Levi's? Now you know. But don't try wearing tight Levi's on bike rides; the seams are in the right places for horse saddles, not bicycle saddles.

C R M Next, adjust the bike seat so it's close to level and neither too high nor too low, and then change your hand position on the handlebars as you ride, so you can sit in different places, forward and back on the seat, resting your weight on slightly different parts of that tender region of your anatomy. This is not easy to do with standard flat handlebars; if you have bar ends, use them; if not, you can often ride smooth sections of trail or road with your hands turned upside down (palm up), or wrapped around the ends of the bars, or hanging on to the brake levers, so you can move a bit on the seat. Even just bending your elbows a lot as you ride downhill will change your body position enough to give your seater some relief.

C R M When you get home, you might spend some of your recovery time looking for a new seat. Some people like the ones with extra padding bulges at the points where the two pelvic bones meet the seat. For some, it's better to have a seat with small gaps in the hard underlying shell, such as the Terry saddles. Others like the ones with little pockets of gel for their bony points (wow, this is starting to sound kinky). Whatever padding you get on a seat, though, make sure it is just at the points where your pelvis rests; the front portion of the seat needs to be narrow and virtually unpadded, so you don't chafe your upper thighs on it as you pedal. That rules out sheepskin seat covers. They're OK for very short trips to the market, but not for real distance biking. And while we're talking tough, remember that the best prevention for a sore seater is not just having a good bike seat, but taking lots of short rides on it so *your* seater gets tough.

CHAPTER 8

Power Train

DESCRIPTION AND DIAGNOSIS: Ⓜ Ⓡ The power train is what delivers your pedal power to the rear wheel. The front half of the system consists of the pedals, the cranks, the bottom-bracket set, the front chainrings (sprockets), and the front changer (derailleur). Between the front and back halves of the power train runs a messy, oily chain. The back half of the system consists of the rear sprockets or cogs (on a freewheel or cassette) and a rear changer (derailleur).

Ⓒ On cruiser bikes, the power train is more simple: one front sprocket or chainring, one rear sprocket or cog, and a chain between them with no derailleurs. For problems with the back half of a cruiser power train, see the *Coaster Brake* section of Chapter 2.

Ⓒ Ⓡ Ⓜ When you have a power train problem, first find out which half of the thing is acting up, then zero in on the individual part that's ailing and fix it. Don't just start fiddling with any part that comes to mind; you can spend hours trying to fix things that are OK before you start solving your actual problem.

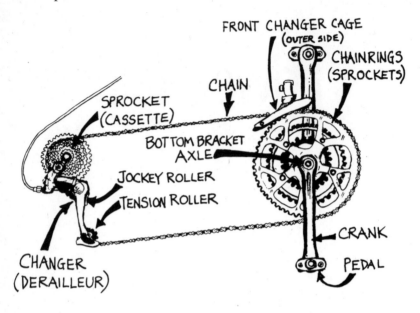

FRONT CHANGER CAGE (OUTER SIDE)

CHAINRINGS (SPROCKETS)

CHAIN

SPROCKET (CASSETTE)

BOTTOM BRACKET AXLE

JOCKEY ROLLER

TENSION ROLLER

CHANGER (DERAILLEUR)

CRANK

PEDAL

8-1 Power Train

C R M Here's a little trick to keep in mind no matter what your power train problem. If you can't solve the problem and you're out in the middle of nowhere, there is a way to get home on your powerless bike, as long as you have a cycling friend and a spare tube along. Simply loop your spare over your friend's seat post and hold onto it so he or she can tow you. If the two of you are about the same size or if you are larger, you should offer to do at least half of the towing work, and let your friend have the free ride. It's hard work on the uphills, but it sure beats walking. How thankful I have been for the help of Bryan, my backwoods cycling companion over the years. You're a true gentleman, Bryan, even if you did want to kill me that time I got us lost in Dead Man's Gulch.

C R M Diagnosis of power train problems involves listening to the bike as you ride it. If there are nasty *grinding, rubbing, squeaking, kerchunking, clinking, or clunking noises* when you pedal, make this simple test: get going at a good clip on a quiet, level place or a slight downhill with smooth ground, then coast and listen. If the nasty noises do not stop when you stop pedaling, your problem is in a wheel, not the power train. See Wheel PROBLEMS and check for brake *stickies* (page 30) too.

C R M If a nasty noise appears only when you pedal, see if it repeats itself, and how often. If it repeats once each time your pedal makes a revolution, then it's probably a front half problem (Chapter 9). If it repeats itself approximately once for every two revolutions of your pedal, then you have a chain problem; go directly to Chain PROBLEMS on page 169. If the noise repeats two to three times for every revolution of the pedal, you probably have a back half problem; see Rear Sprocket PROBLEMS (page 180) or Rear Changer PROBLEMS (page 186). If the noise you get is constant, unvarying, it might be any of the parts of the power train. Stop the bike, hang it up or have a friend hold it up, and listen to each part of the power train as you turn the pedals by hand. Two common steady noises are a squeaky chain and grindy rear-changer rollers. When you have isolated the problem area, turn to the section that covers it so you can zero in on the specific trouble.

M R If your *gears slip* or change by themselves, there's something wrong with the gear control lever or cable adjustment. See *gear slippage* on page 186.

M R If the chain keeps flying off the front sprockets, or if the chain is always rubbing the front changer, see Gear Changer PROBLEMS on page 186. On the other hand, if the chain keeps getting sucked into the space between the front sprockets and the chainstay, see ***chain sucking*** on page 172.

[M] [R] If you hear a plunk-plunking noise when you're in a low gear and the chain is on the largest of the rear sprockets, STOP RIDING! That innocuous little sound is a warning that the rear changer (derailleur) is badly out of adjustment or alignment, and it is about to self-destruct in the rear wheel spokes. See ***changer system adjustment*** on page 188 to save the thing from certain death.

CHAPTER 9

Front Half of Power Train

DESCRIPTION AND DIAGNOSIS: **C** **R** **M** The front half of the power train consists of the pedals, the cranks, the bottom bracket set, the front sprocket(s) or chainwheel(s), and, if you have a mountain or road bike, a front changer (See Illustration 8-1). The front changer is not included in this section, however; it is under *Gear Changers* on page 206.

M **R** If you have a problem with the front half of your power train, you have to find out where it is, then go to the section about the ailing unit. If your chain is throwing or your front changer rubs on the chain all the time, however, just go straight to *Gear Changer* PROBLEMS. They're on page 186, with the rest of the stuff on changers. If your chain is sucking all the time, see Chain PROBLEMS on page 172.

C R M If your chain goes *kerchunk* and jumps up each time it hits a certain point of the front sprocket, see *Front Sprocket or Chainring* PROBLEMS. If you hear nasty noises, like clicks, clunks, or harsh squeaks at each revolution of the pedal, first check the pedal itself. Is it hard to revolve on its spindle by hand? Is it really loose on the spindle? Is it obviously bent or bashed? When you spin it by hand, does it catch and stick on its bearings? Has the dust cap flown off, letting muck and grit into the bearings? Look at Illustration 9-1 to get oriented, then see *Pedals* PROBLEMS.

C R M If you hear a clunk, creak, or sharp squeak each time you push down on one pedal or the other, or if you sometimes feel a slight slippage of a pedal as you push hard on it, or if one of the cranks is knocking on the frame, see *Cranks* PROBLEMS. If you fix the cranks and still hear a squeak, check for loose chainring mounting bolts, then check the pedal to see if it has come loose in the crank, then check the pedal bearings, then check the bottom-bracket bearings. Sometimes front half squeaks are hard to chase down.

C R M If you hear grinding noises that you can't pin down on the pedals, or if your whole front half can slip back and forth and wiggle in the frame, or if the whole front half is hard to turn, see *Bottom Bracket* PROBLEMS.

Pedals

DESCRIPTION: C R M What you push on with your feet to make the bike go. A pedal consists of a metal, plastic, or metal and rubber platform, a spindle that is screwed into the crank, and bearing sets on which the platform revolves around the spindle. There is often a dust cap screwed or wedged onto the pedal platform, protecting the bearings (see Illustration 9-2). There are also sealed-bearing pedals. Mountain bikes often have a large, removable platform that you can replace if it gets bent or broken. If you ride hard, it will. Road bikes and pricey mountain bikes often have clipless pedals, which require special cleats attached to the bottoms of your cycling shoes.

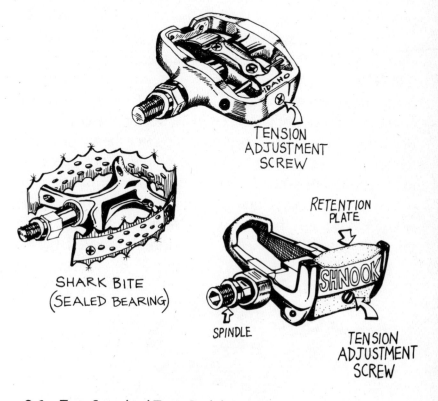

9-1 Top: Standard Type Pedal; Bottom: Clipless Type Pedal

PROBLEMS: **C** **R** **M** *Pedals loose or tight and noisy.* First make sure the spindle is screwed tightly into the crank. If it's loose, you need to get a wrench that'll fit tight on those two flats that are on the spindle right next to where it screws into the crank; the Cool Tool adjustable wrench will do the trick, though it doesn't give you much leverage; the same is true of a 15-mm or ⁹⁄₁₆-inch hub spanner. Some pedals have wide flats so you can use a standard open-end wrench. Keep in mind, as you tighten, that the left pedal has left-hand threads, which means that you turn the spindle *counterclockwise* to tighten it. Tighten the right pedal spindle clockwise, like normal threaded parts. If you can't get a loose pedal really tight, just keep an eye on it as you ride home, then get an official pedal spanner and really honk on it for maximum tightness (just don't overdo it and strip those aluminum threads out of the crank).

C R M If your pedal is hard to turn, or slops around and makes noise when you turn it, check the bearings. You can't check them on most clipless pedals, but on the pedals with platforms, if the pedal has a dust cap over the outer end of the spindle, see if it has an Allen-key hole. If not, see if it is loose enough to take off with your hands or a pair of wide pliers or something. When you get the dust cap off, look inside. Do you see the end of the spindle and a nut that's threaded onto it? That means the bearings are adjustable. Or

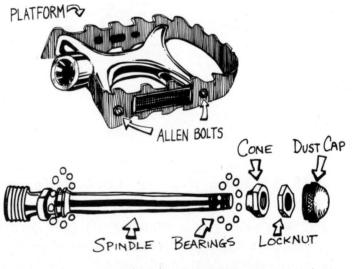

9-2 Pedal, Exploded View

is there a sealed bearing (a black ring-shaped thing) with no nut in sight? That means you have sealed, nonadjustable bearings, and they are shot. All you can do is ride home and get a shop to replace them, or replace the whole pedal.

C R M If the bearings are adjustable, see if you can back off (c-cl) the locknut on the end of the spindle by sticking your adjustable wrench jaws in there end-wise. Many pedals don't give you enough room to get in there; you may want to just oil the bearings and ride home to take on the adjustment hassle there.

M If you decide to adjust the bearings on a mountain bike pedal and you're out on the trail, you may have to undo (c-cl) the Allen bolts holding the platform to the pedal and remove the platform to get it out of your way. Then take off the dust cap and loosen (c-cl) the locknut.

C R M If the pedal is loose, tighten (cl) the cone with a screwdriver: stick the screwdriver in along the outer wall of the bearing housing and slide it around (cl) until it catches on one of the flats of the cone and tightens it. Then tighten (cl) the locknut. Put a drop of oil in there and try to get a drop into the bearings at the other end of the pedal, too.

C R M If the pedal is tight (hard to turn), adjust the cone (c-cl) to make it a little looser. As with all bearings, these should be set so there is very little "play" or wiggle-room; just enough to let the little balls roll around freely. When the bearings are adjusted right, tighten (cl) the locknut and then tighten (cl) the dust cap in again. Put the platform on again if you took it off.

C R M If the pedal still makes noise and refuses to turn smoothly on the spindle, the bearings are probably shot. Read ***Pedal bent, bashed, or broken***, below, and replace your pedal.

C R M ***Pedal bent, bashed, or broken.*** If you're out in the boonies, you have to limp home or to a bike shop as well as you can. In many cases you can use the other foot

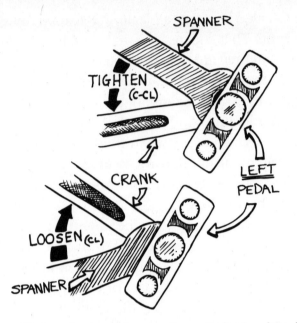

9-3   Tightening and Loosening a Left-Hand Pedal

to do the work of pedaling, and just give the mashed pedal a light push as it is going down, in order to get your usable pedal back up to the top of its stroke so you can heave down on it again. If you make it to a shop or home, use a pedal spanner to remove the shot pedal. The spindle unscrews counterclockwise on the right pedal, clockwise on the left. (See Illustration 9-3 to get the idea.) Notice how the spanner makes a "closing V" with the crank; this formation gives you maximum leverage for loosening or tightening a pedal on a crank.

C R M Make sure the threaded end of the new pedal is the right size, and that the threads are of the same type as those on your old pedal. Pedals from some countries don't fit in cranks from other countries. Tighten (cl on the right pedal, c-cl on the left) the new pedal in thoroughly, and you're on your way.

M R ***Clipless pedal retention plate loose:*** Your shoe slips around in the retention plate of your clipless pedal. First check to make sure the screws holding the cleat to your shoe are tight (cl). Adjust the position of the cleat so your heel just misses the crank as it spins by, then tighten (cl) the cleat screws thoroughly. If your shoe has a very sharply curved sole so the cleat can't fit flat against it, put a little shim (flat piece of metal) or a dime under the front end before you tighten the screw down. If the cleat is worn down from walking on it, mark the place where the cleat is on your shoe (trace around it with a pen), then take the screws out. Notice which length screws go in which holes, and put them back in the same holes. Get a new cleat just like the old one. When mounting it, make sure the screws go into the same holes they came out of.

M R Usually, fixing up the cleat will take care of your loose clipless pedal. If not, you have to adjust or replace the retention plate. Most clipless pedals have an adjusting screw; other types require replacement when they get too loose.

M R To adjust the spring tension on the pedals like the ones in Illustration 9-1, turn the adjusting screw in (cl). GO EASY! Whether you have a big screw, like the one shown in Illustration 9-1, or a screw with an Allen head, or a little adjusting screw on the top surface of the pedal, you have to turn that screw carefully, to avoid stripping the threads. Don't turn it too far in either direction. On the big-screw type, you have about 2½ turns from minimum tension to all the way tight. Some of the little-screw types only allow about a single turn from minimum to maximum tension. So don't expect to make unlimited changes to the spring tension with that screw. The safest way to do an adjustment on either kind is to turn the screw in (cl) all the way, GENTLY, without forcing it when it reaches the end of its range. Then try the tension and loosen (c-cl) the screw a little at a time if you need to. Make sure you do not loosen the big-screw type more than 2½ turns. And when you finish adjusting the tension on one pedal, adjust the other one to get them equal.

Ⓜ Ⓡ If you have the big-screw type of retention plate and the plate is really loose or cracked or worn down, you can replace the whole plate by loosening (c-cl) the big screw all the way. Get a kit for your kind of pedal at a bike shop, then put the new plate on carefully, screwing the adjusting screw in until it stops, then backing it off 2½ turns or less. If you have the little-screw type of retention plate and it gets too loose or beat up, you have to take the pedal off and let a shop that carries those pedals do the replacement.

Cranks

DESCRIPTION: Ⓒ Ⓡ Ⓜ The cranks are the sturdy bars or tubes of metal that attach your pedals to the axle of the bottom bracket. The pedal is screwed into the crank. The crank is usually held to the bottom-bracket axle by a bolt that goes through the crank and into the end of the axle, or by a nut on a threaded stud that sticks out from the end of the axle. Cranks of this style are called cotterless, or three-piece. On some American cruisers, the two cranks and the bottom bracket axle are one solid piece of steel. This style of crank is called one-piece, or Ashtabula (ah, such a lovely name). On some European bikes, the cranks are held to the axle by a wedge-shaped cotter pin. Though I'm fond of my old cotter-crank Raleigh, it has become so rare I don't cover cottered cranks in this book; see a shop if you have trouble with loose or bent cottered cranks.

PROBLEMS: Ⓜ Ⓡ *Clunk, creak, or sharp squeak* heard at each revolution of the pedal. You may not even hear any sound, but still feel slippage each time you push down hard

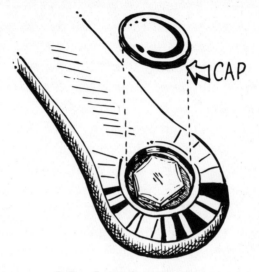

9-4 Cotterless Crank

on one of the pedals. Either symptom probably indicates that your ***crank is loose*** where it attaches to the thick axle that goes through the bottom bracket in the frame. Don't ride the bike with a loose crank!

M R You need a socket tool or a crank-bolt-tightening tool to tighten up your crank; if you have a Cool Tool, the socket tool in it will fit most crank bolts. If you don't have a tool for your crank bolt, hobble to the nearest farm shop (amazing how many of them now have metric tools for their Japanese tractors), garage, or bike shop. On your way to acquiring the crank tool, use only the tight crank to pedal. Don't use the loose crank to pedal hard, especially up steep hills. You can easily mess up the crank so much you'll have to buy a new one.

M R When you have a crank tightening tool, do the following test to make *sure* you have a crank problem, and to determine which crank is loose. Get off the bike and lean one bar end against a tree or something, then position the pedals so one is forward and one is back, with the cranks horizontal. Get the weight of your upper body positioned over the top tube, directly over the pedals, and rest one hand on each pedal. This may require sticking one hand, arm, and shoulder through the diamond of the frame, but most mountain bike frames are small enough you can reach over the top tube.

M R When you're all set, push down sharply on both pedals at the same time with your hands, putting all your weight behind the push. Feel anything give? Watch the joint of each crank and the bottom-bracket axle as you push down, in order to determine which crank is loose. You may have to rotate the cranks 180 degrees and do the test again. It may take three or four tests, or you may not be able to tell accurately which crank is loose. But if you feel that give or hear the squeak of the crank shifting on its axle, tighten the crank bolt you suspect most, and tighten both bolts if you're not sure which one is loose.

M R To tighten your crank, first remove the dust cap over the crank bolt. Usually you have to unscrew (c-cl) them by putting something pointed in two little holes and twisting carefully (use the needlenoses of needlenose pliers, or two tiny Allen keys, or two little nails, or the ends of a paper clip—whatever you can scrounge up; I even used a barb on a barbed wire fence once). Some dust caps require that you pop them out by sticking a screwdriver or knife blade in a little slot at the edge. Take care not to destroy the threads in the crank that are under the dust cap, whatever you do. Those threads are crucial for crank removal.

M R When you have the dust cap off, fit the socket tool over the bolt head or nut inside the crank. Make sure the tool fits well. If you are using the socket tool that's part of your Cool Tool, make sure it is snug on the crank bolt or nut, then fit the adjustable wrench on the flats of the socket and hold the socket in place with your thumb while you turn the wrench. Tighten (cl) the bolt or nut thoroughly.

When it gets hard to turn the wrench, place it on the bolt or nut in such a way that you are making a "closing V" with the tool handle and the crank; the idea is to set things up so you can grip the crank and the wrench handle with the same hand. (See Illustration 9-3 to get the idea.) You can get the bolt or nut very tight by this method if you take it slow and steady. Just make sure you don't apply so much oomph and leverage to the wrench that you strip the threads on the bolt or nut.

M R When your crank bolt or nut is tight, you can ride in peace. You can put the dust cap back on if you want, but I prefer to leave them off. Dust never hurts the crank bolt or nut. And while I'm giving opinions, I gotta say I hate it when they use nuts to hold the cranks on. If you have nuts holding your cranks on, and one or both of them came loose, make a mental note to get some thread glue (like Loctite) when you get home, and take both nuts off, apply glue to their threads, then re-tighten (cl) them so they'll stay tight (if you're lucky). If you have lots of trouble with these nuts coming loose, take the whole bottom bracket set apart and replace the axle (or spindle, as many people call it) with the kind of axle that accepts crank bolts. Then throw your nut-type axle, and the nuts, in a recycling bin. Humph. I hope they make flimsy car parts out of them, as a bad karma reward.

C R M *Crank bent, knocking chainstay.* If you've had a wreck and banged a pedal so hard the crank is bent and hits against the chainstay, there isn't much you can do with your portable tool kit. There is a last-ditch method you can try for a temporary fix to get you home, though, if you can just find a farm shop with a huge (18- to 24-inch) adjustable wrench. Either walk or get a tow (see page 144) to the farm, then take the pedal off the bent crank (see page 151). Wrap some heavy cloth or burlap around the end of the crank.

Then turn the crank so it is pointing straight up, and lay the bike down gently on the other side from the one with the bent crank.

C R M Adjust the big wrench so the jaws fit snugly over the padded end of the crank. Make sure the jaws won't dig into the threaded hole for the pedal spindle. Hold the top tube of the bike down with one hand, and use the other hand to lever the handle of the wrench upward, slowly and steadily straightening the crank. If it is a strong crank, it'll take a lot of spaghetti power on that wrench. You may even have to ask a friend or a farmer to help hold the bike down while you do the bending. But do it slowly, so you don't snap the crank off or bend it too far.

C R M When the crank is fairly close to straight, put the pedal back on, then make a mental note to take the bike to a good shop for professional straightening, or replace the crank when you get home. A bent and rebent crank is much weaker than a new one (though I must confess, I rode a rebent steel Magistroni crank on my old Cinelli for years).

M R *Crank ruined; replacement*. This procedure is for all bikes except cruisers with one-piece (Ashtabula) cranks. If you are replacing a right crank, get the chain off the front sprocket and out of the way. Then, on either the right or left crank, unscrew or pop off the dust cap. Remove (c-cl) the crank bolt or nut, using a socket wrench or the socket end of your crank-remover tool. Next back (c-cl) the inner post of the remover all the way out. Thread (cl) the whole remover all the way into the dust cap threads.

M R Put a socket wrench over the hex head of the remover post. Screw in (cl) the post until it pushes against the axle, loosening the crank. If the crank won't loosen, tap gently on the end of the remover with a hammer, then tighten (cl) the post a bit, then tap and tighten again. When the crank does come loose, pull it straight off the end of the axle. Remove the remover (c-cl) from the dust cap threads in the crank. If the threads in the crank get stripped in spite of all your precautions, and the crank is still stuck on the axle, go to a good machine shop and see if they can get it off with a gear puller. Take the old crank, and, if possible, the rest of the bike to a bike shop and get an exact replacement. They cost a lot. Don't be shocked.

🇲 🇷 *To install a new crank,* take the dust cap off (c-cl) if it has one. Clean and dry the square hole in the crank and the square axle end meticulously, then smear some pipe thread compound, like Never-seez, on the flat surfaces on the square end of the axle. Line the crank up so it's opposite the other one (unless you want to try a revolutionary pedaling cadence), and gently slip it onto the axle. Be careful at this juncture. If you misshape the square hole in the soft metal of your new crank, it will never stay tight, and you will have wasted a lot of money replacing your old one. Get the bolt and washer or the nut, and start (cl) the fastener onto the axle with your fingers. If you have a nut fastener, you might want to clean the threads in it and on the stud with degreaser, then put a thread glue like Loctite on the threads, so the bugger will stay tight.

🇲 🇷 When you have turned the fastener down inside the crank so far you can't reach it with your fingers, put on the installer socket or other socket tool and screw in (cl) the bolt or nut so it's snug. *Don't* tighten it yet. Shift the crank back and forth slightly on the axle when the bolt is snug, then tighten the bolt or nut a bit at a time, making sure the crank is seating properly on the axle. Get the fastener good and tight. Screw in (cl) the dust cap and replace the chain on the sprocket if it's a right crank you replaced. After fifty miles of riding, check the fastener and tighten it again if it can be tightened.

Bottom Bracket

DESCRIPTION: C R M The bottom bracket is the part of the bike that holds the cranks in the frame and lets them spin freely. It consists of a heavy axle or spindle (on the Ashtabula setup, the axle is just the middle portion of the one-piece crank), bearings, a fixed and an adjustable bearing cup, and a lockring for the adjustable bearing cup. (see Illustration 9-5). There are also great sealed-bearing bottom bracket sets, made for cotterless crank sets. One note about sealed bearing sets, though: New ones can get a bit loose— just get a shop to tighten the threaded ring that holds the whole unit in your bike frame.

PROBLEMS: C R M *Bottom bracket loose or tight.* Either your whole bottom-bracket axle (spindle) is loose, so it jiggles from side to side when you pedal, or it is hard to turn the cranks at all.

M R If you have a sealed bottom bracket (there is no adjustable race and lockring on the left side), the mounting sleeves must be loose. Take the bike to the shop that sold you the bike or installed the sealed bottom bracket. Ask them to tighten the thing up with their special tools and savvy. If they do a good job, it shouldn't come loose again.

M R If you have a non-sealed bottom bracket, as shown in Illustration 9-5, you have to adjust the adjustable bearing race on the left side of the bottom bracket. First use a bottom bracket spanner to loosen (c-cl) the lockring. If you're out on the trail or road, take a screwdriver and set the end in one of the notches in the lockring. Tap the screwdriver with a rock, aiming the screwdriver counterclockwise to loosen the ring. When the ring is loose, take a small Allen key or something like that and put it in one of the small holes that are set into the end of the adjustable race or bearing cup. Turn the thing the way you need to in order to tighten (cl) or loosen (c-cl) it. The best way is to tighten (cl) it all the way in until it's hard to turn the cranks, then back off (c-cl) the adjustable race about an eighth of a turn. Then tighten (cl) the lockring by using the spanner or screwdriver in a notch again.

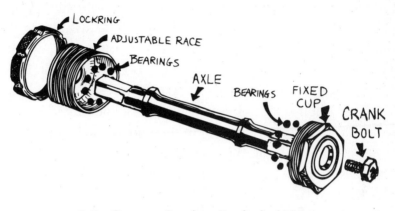

9-5 Bottom Bracket, Exploded View

M R If the bottom bracket gets jiggly again soon, your fixed cup is probably loose. All you can do out in the backcountry is turn it in with your fingers or maybe narrow-jawed channel-lock pliers, if you can borrow pliers from a farmer or garage. The fixed cup tightens clockwise on some bikes, but counterclockwise on most others, so you have to figure out which way works on yours and get it as tight as you can manage, then ride home, keeping an eye on it. Once home, tighten it up with a spanner that fits in there, or take it to a shop that will have the proper spanner for the job.

C If you have a cruiser bike with a one-piece (Ashtabula) crank and it is loose or tight, you have to loosen (c-cl) the locknut on the left side of the crankset, then tighten (cl) the bearing race under the locknut, pushing it around with a screwdriver in the slot if it's hard to turn. When it gets tight on the bearings, back it off about an eighth of a turn, then tighten (cl) the locknut, and you're set to go.

C R M *Bottom bracket noisy:* If you have grindy, crackly noises coming from the front half of your power train, and you can't trace them to the pedals or cranks, chances are they are being made by grit or worn parts inside the bottom bracket. If you have some lubricant and the bearings are not sealed (you can see a little space between the bottom-bracket axle and the bearing race), work a couple of drops into each side of the bottom bracket. It may help to squirt the oil into that space between the axle and the race, then tip the bike so the lubricant runs down the axle into the works as you spin the cranks backward. When you get some lube in there and the noises quiet down, ride home in peace, but replace the whole bottom bracket set (bearings and axle) when you get a chance; the best idea is to have a shop install a sealed bottom bracket set. Those things can really last; I had a Phil Wood one that lasted eighteen years, and it even took a trip to the bottom of the bay when my bike fell off a pier.

C If you have a cruiser with noisy bottom bracket bearings, you can't get a sealed replacement. They don't make sealed bearings for those good old one-piece Ashtabula cranksets. To **overhaul a one-piece crank bottom bracket** like those on most cruisers, start by unscrewing (clockwise, remember) the left pedal and taking the chain off the front sprocket. Then get a big wrench, like a Ford monkey wrench or a big adjustable-end wrench if you have one. The channel lock will do if you're careful. Get a good grip on the big locknut that's around the crank on the left side of the bottom bracket, hold the right crank with your other hand, and loosen (clockwise—that's backward) that big nut.

C Put the big nut and the washer under it in a jar. Unscrew (cl) the wide left-bearing cone. It's the next thing screwed onto the bottom-bracket axle. It has two slots in it. Start unscrewing it (cl) with a screwdriver in one of the slots if necessary, then spin it out with your fingers. Hold the crank in place against the right set bearing cone, and screw (cl) the left bearing cone off the left end of the crank. Put the left cone in the jar. Take out the ball bearings, leaving them in their retainer, and put them in the jar, too. Then move the crank-axle unit to the right, tipping it as you go, and ease the whole piece all the way out of the frame through the bottom bracket. Remove the ball bearings—still in their retainer—from the right side and put them in the jar.

C Look at all the bearing cups and cones. (The cups are set into the bottom-bracket shell, and the right cone is screwed onto the axle.) If any of the bearing surfaces are pitted, or if the balls themselves are scored, or if any of the balls are missing, take the parts to a good bike shop and get exact replacements. If you need to get a cup out of the bottom-bracket shell, stick the big screwdriver through the shell from the opposite side, set the tip of the blade against the rim of the cup in there and tap, working your way around the rim to drive the cup out evenly. Using solvent and rags, thoroughly clean and dry the parts you don't replace.

C *To reconstruct a dismantled one-piece crank bottom-bracket set,* first screw (cl) the right cone (if you had to take it off) onto the crank. Squeeze bearing grease into the bearing retainers so that all the spaces around the balls are filled with grease. Wipe excess grease off the outside of the retainer rings and set them down on something *very clean* within arm's reach of your bottom bracket. Put one of the bearing retainers onto the crank. Remember that the solid ring side of the retainer goes against the cone. If you put a new cup in the bottom bracket shell, make sure it is well seated. Tap around and around its edges to get it all the way in.

C Take the right crank in your right hand and stick the left crank through without forcing anything. Now put the bearings over the left crank and follow them with the left cone. Remember, the left cone screws on counterclockwise. Tighten the left cone up on the bearings, then back it off (cl) about an eighth of a turn, or until the crank turns smoothly but doesn't wiggle. Put on the washer, then tighten up the big locknut. Get that nut good and tight, then check to make sure the cranks are still adjusted correctly. Put your left pedal back on (c-cl), get the chain back on the front sprocket, and you're set to go.

Front Sprocket or Chainring

DESCRIPTION: C R M The round metal wheel with all the points around it that pulls the chain when you pedal. On some cruiser bikes, the front sprocket is permanently attached to the right crank. On multispeed bikes, the right crank usually has three or five arms, onto which the chainrings are bolted. (See Illustration 9-6.)

PROBLEMS: C R M There's a *kerchunk* sound every time the pedals go around, or the chain falls off every time it gets to a certain place on the chainring. Get the bike hung up on a fence post, a low limb on a tree (use a spare tube to tie it up if you need to), or your friend's willing hands. Crank the pedals slowly and watch the chain as it feeds onto the top of the front sprocket (chainring). Does the chain kick up or jump off when it gets to one of the teeth of the sprocket each time that one tooth comes around? If so, you have a bent sprocket tooth.

C R M If the chain doesn't kick up on any one tooth, continue cranking slowly and watch the chain where it goes over the rear sprocket, or through the rollers on the rear changer. Does the chain kick up or jump a little back there

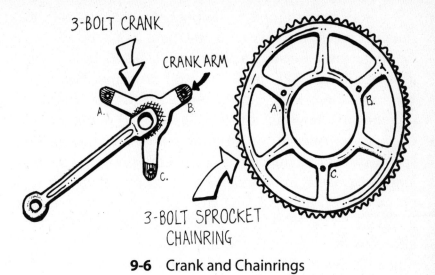

3-BOLT CRANK

CRANK ARM

A.   B.

C.

3-BOLT SPROCKET
CHAINRING

A.   B.

C.

9-6   Crank and Chainrings

every once in a while? Look closely at the chain where it jumps. Is a link of the chain stuck so it doesn't flex and then straighten as it goes through the rollers? See Chain PROBLEMS if that is the case. Is the chain kicking up on one tooth of the freewheel or cassette sprockets (cogs)? If so, see Rear Sprocket PROBLEMS.

🅲 🆁 🅼 If you have a ***bent tooth*** on your front sprocket or chainring, you have to play dentist. Mark the tooth that the chain kicks up on, or jumps off of. You can just make a fingernail mark in the grease if you don't have a marker handy.

🅲 🆁 🅼 Take the chain off the chainring, then spin the cranks slowly and look down from directly above the chainring. Watch that you don't bonk your chin with a pedal, but also watch closely for the marked tooth as it comes over the top of the chainring. Can you see which way it's bent compared to the ones on either side? If you can't see any bend in the tooth, look at it from the side of the bike. If it's chipped or badly worn down, you'll have to ride home or to a good bike shop to replace the whole chainring, as described below.

If you find that a tooth is simply bent a little to one side, put your adjustable wrench on the bent tooth and tighten it up so the jaws are snug against both sides. Bend the tooth a bit at a time. Take the wrench off now and then to see how you are doing. If the sprocket is a high-quality forged-aluminum one, it will be hard to bend, but you can do it with patience and a firm but steady touch. Steel sprocket teeth are much easier to bend, but some have all kinds of tweaks and bends in them to start with, for supposed ease of shifting. In this case, you have to try to imitate the bends of the other teeth around the sprocket. If, in your efforts to straighten one tooth, you bend the whole chainring a bit, see *front sprocket wobbles,* below.

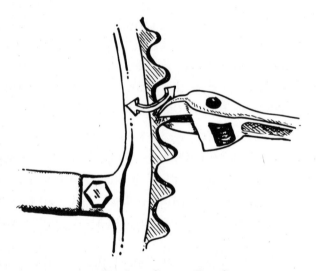

9-7   Bending a Tooth

When you get the tooth straight, put the chain back on and try the slow pedaling test again. If the chain runs smoothly, congrats! If not, check for another bent tooth or maybe a tight link in the chain.

Ⓜ Ⓡ To *replace a chainring,* on most mountain and road bikes, all you have to do is take the chain off it, then undo (c-cl) the Allen bolts that hold the chainring to the crank. Then take the ring off, put the new one on, and tighten (cl) all the Allen bolts back on. Make sure you get any washers back where they came from in the process.

C To ***replace a chainring on a one-piece crank,*** you have to do the overhaul procedure on page 162, and when you get the one-piece crank out of the bottom bracket, take the chainring off and replace it. Then do the reconstruction procedure on page 163. Whew. Quite a project, just to change a chainring.

C R M ***Front sprocket wobbles.*** This is an annoying problem. It means that one side of the chain or the other always rubs the cage of the front gear changer, no matter how well you adjust the thing. Prop the bike up so it won't fall over, then crank the pedals backward slowly while you look down on the chainrings from above. Find the area of the sprocket that bends in or out and makes the chain rub the changer cage. Mark the bent area of the sprocket, with some grease from the chain if you don't have a marker with you. Sometimes it's hard to tell whether the chainring is bent in on one side, or out on the other. Try to decide where the majority of the chainring is, and call the rest bent. Does the bent area you marked fall near one of the crank arms that hold the chainring to the crank? Usually a bent chainring has been caused by a bent crank arm (spider) or a bad connection between the arm and the chainring (see Illustration 9-6).

C R M If you are out on the trail or road, first make sure all the bolts that hold the chainring to the crank arms are tight. Then find a chunk of wood that will butt up against the side of the crank arm where your bend is. A short section of a tree limb that has been sawed for firewood is ideal; a hunk of two-by-four is great, too, but I don't ride around construction projects if I can help it. Place one end of your chunk of wood against the crank arm that is bent, then give the other end of the chunk of wood a solid whack with a fist-sized rock. You may have to lay the bike down on one side to do this properly. Check to see if you've straightened the chainring after your first whack. Rotate the cranks a bit if you have to take another whack, so you don't wreck the bottom-bracket bearings.

C R M If a minor wobble persists, you may have to do some multi-tooth dental work with your adjustable wrench, as described in the ***bent tooth*** section above; just push the jaws of the adjustable wrench on further than you did to straighten a single tooth. If you get the chainring close to straight but not perfect, don't worry about it. As long as the chain doesn't throw or rub on the changer every time it goes around, you've done a good job.

C R M If you are at home, you can use a block of hard wood and a hammer for the above procedure, or you can get a great big screwdriver and use it (*gently* now, gently) as a lever to straighten out the bent arm of the chainring set. To pry the chainring arm *out*, set the tip of the screwdriver blade against the outer side of the bottom bracket. Hook the tip of the screwdriver inside the crank arm or the innermost chainring to bend a chainring arm *in*. Go easy. Make sure the shank of the screwdriver is pushing against one of the arms of the chainring; if you miss, you can make a sharp, unfixable bend in the chainring.

CHAPTER 10

Chain

DESCRIPTION: C R M The dirtiest part of the bike. It has rollers riveted to connecting plates and connects the front and rear sprockets. (See Illustration 8-1.) There are several different standard sizes, none of which are interchangeable. On most cruisers, one link—the master link—has a U-shaped or oversized plate on one side that can be popped on and off. (See Illustration 10-1.) Bikes with derailleurs do not have master links.

PROBLEMS: C R M *Chain thrown.* Your chain has come off the chainring and/or the rear sprocket. You probably need to adjust your gear changers, but use this section to get your chain back on the sprockets and to check the chain for looseness and lack of lubricant.

M R If the chain is jammed on either side of the freewheel or cassette sprockets, you have to grab (yuch!) the upper section of chain, just forward from those rear sprockets, then yank up as you slowly rotate the rear wheel forward. You can do this by rolling the bike forward slowly as you pull the chain free. If the chain threw off the highest (smallest) sprocket, you may have to loosen the rear wheel quick-release to free the jammed chain.

M **R** To get your chain back on the bike, put it on the rear sprocket first. Put the rear changer in its high gear position, then make sure the chain goes through both of the rollers, making a backward "S" shape. Get it to run from the top roller onto the smallest sprocket, and all the way around that sprocket so it goes straight forward off the top. Put a friend's bike in high gear and take a look if you're not sure how it should look.

C **R** **M** When the chain is set on the smallest rear sprocket, pull the length of chain that comes off the top of the rear sprocket tight, then press a couple of links down over the teeth at the top of the front sprocket or chainring. Crank the pedals forward with one hand while holding the links on the chainring teeth with the other hand. You have to walk along next to the bike as it rolls forward. The rest of the chain will pop onto that chainring.

C **R** **M** Read the rest of the PROBLEMS in this section and find out what made the chain jump off. If the chain is OK,

10-1 Master Link

check your gear changer adjustment, then check the front and rear sprockets for wobbles or damaged teeth.

🅒 🅡 🅜 *Squeaky or gunky chain.* You haven't lubricated or cleaned it in a while. It's easy to forget. But you pay heavily for that negligence on a long ride; a dry or dirty chain wastes a lot of your energy. I remember once when we were miles from nowhere and my chain went completely dry after the third creek crossing. I stopped at my friend Steve's secluded cabin and found that there was no proper chain lubricant of any kind. But his partner, Anne, let me use some of her olive oil. What a difference! Viva la Italiana!

🅒 🅡 🅜 Before putting lubricant on the chain, see how dirty it is. If it is coated with mud or grime and the stuff is not dry, take a rag or the edge of your shirttail, hold it loosely around the top section of chain between the front and rear sprockets, and run the pedals backward so the chain slides through the cleaning rag. This'll usually take enough of the gunk off to make the chain usable.

🅜 🅡 To lubricate the chain, get out your bike lubricant if you have some, or borrow a can of light motor oil from a farmer or garage (everybody has their own favorite lubricant, but plain old oil works OK in a pinch). Lie the bike down on its left side, then raise the back end of the bike, so it sticks straight up while the front wheel is still lying on its side. Hold onto a seat stay with one hand (keep your fingers out of the spokes!), then spin the back wheel backward, so the chain feeds backward over the rear sprocket and through the rollers.

🅜 🅡 While the chain is feeding over the rear sprocket, dribble lubricant on it. If it slows to a stop, give the back wheel another backward spin and dribble more lubricant on, until you're sure all the links of the chain have gotten a dose. Squirt a bit of lube in each roller where it spins on its axle. You don't have to work the lubricant in or anything;

that'll happen as you ride. In fact, if there's extra oil dripping off the chain, wipe it off with a rag; extra lubricant picks up dust and grit, which can raise the coefficient of friction higher than the oil lowers it.

C If you have a cruiser with a dry or rusty chain, you can turn the bike upside down and pedal the thing forward as you drip oil on the chain where it passes over the chainring. Messy, but it works.

C **R** **M** When you get back on the bike after lubricating the chain, you'll notice an incredible improvement in the ease of pedaling and gear shifting. Remember that. Keep the chain lubricated from now on. And clean the chain with a wire brush when you get home from any particularly muddy or gritty ride.

M *Chain sucking.* This variation on a thrown chain usually happens when you are having lots of fun. That means, you are going fast, getting squirrely, drifting half out of control, giggling as you pedal for all you are worth. Then, all of a sudden, GRRAAACK! The chain gets sucked between the innermost chainring and the chain stay.

M It's a drag when it happens. In fact, it sucks. If the chain stays stuck in there when you stop pedaling, back-pedal and it should pop free.

M A number of things can cause chain suckage, but the most common causes are loose chain flapping around, or a bent sprocket, or the use of inappropriate gears. First off, don't use the smallest chainring when you are riding downhill. It makes the chain run loose, and puts it in very close proximity to the chain-suckage danger area, that narrow gap between the small chainring and the chainstay. Next, check your chainrings for wobbles or bent teeth. (See pages 167–170.) If you have oval chainrings, ride home carefully, then consider changing those oval chainrings for round ones. Oval chainrings increase chain flap.

M R *Chain death.* The chain falls between two of the chainrings and gets stuck in there. This is usually due to one of two problems: either you are using a narrow chain and chainrings made for a wider chain, or your chainrings are either bent or not bolted together properly, so there is a gap between them. You can fix a bent or loose chainring (see Front Sprocket PROBLEMS), but if the chainrings and chain are mismatched sizes, you gotta ride home slow and easy, then go to a shop and replace one or the other.

M R *Loose chain.* Your chain sags down between the front and rear sprockets, especially when you are using the small chainring. This is a problem that can lead to chain suckage, chain throwing, chain death, and other masochistic chain acts I refuse to describe. So to get rid of that sag and have a longer, healthier life with your chain, take out a link or two, as described in *tight or bent links,* below. To see how many links you need to remove, put the bike in the gear that runs the chain from the biggest chainring to the biggest rear sprocket. I know folks say that we shouldn't use this gear, but sometimes, in a pinch, we use it, and the bike should be able to accommodate. When you get the bike into this gear, see if you can make a fold in the lower section of the chain between the tension roller and the chainring without stretching the rear changer arm forward all the way to the limit. If you can, take out as many links as you can. Usually it will be no more than a link or two.

C R M *Tight or bent links.* When one part of your chain goes over the rear sprocket (especially a small rear sprocket) and through the rollers, the chain kinks, and then doesn't come unkinked. Or it jumps and kerchunks as it passes over the sprocket. The kink indicates a tight link; the jumping and kerchunking indicates a bent or damaged link of the chain.

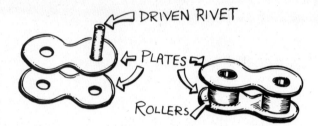

10-2   Two Different Chain Links

C R M If you suspect that you have a ***tight link***, get the bike up off the ground and crank the pedals slowly. Watch the chain as it goes over the rear sprocket and through the rollers. See the chain jump a little each time a particular link comes around? That's your tight link. Flex the jumpy area of the chain with your fingers until you find the link that doesn't want to flex. Mark it with a little scratch on the side plate so you don't lose it among its normal brothers.

Try to loosen the tight link up by putting a little lubricant on it and working it back and forth with your fingers. Flex it not only up and down, but side to side, so you loosen up the joints between the rivets and the rollers.

C R M Look closely at the tight link and the ones around it. Is there a twist in the chain at your tight link? If so, get two adjustable wrenches (you *are* riding with a friend who's got one, I hope) and adjust the wrenches carefully so they squeeze the side plates of the links to either side of the twisted one. Then twist the two wrenches gently, against the bend, so it straightens out. It's amazing how often you can get the thing pretty close to straight, or at least straight enough to loosen up the tight link and ride home without throwing your chain over and over.

C R M If you can't get your tight link loose by the above methods, get out your chain tool and set the rivet of the tight link in the slot on the chain tool that's for spreading

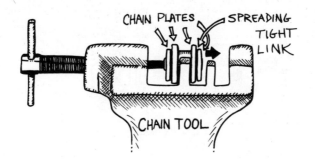

10-3 Chain Tool Spreading Tight Link

links, as shown in Illustration 10-3. Turn the point of the tool in (cl) until it pushes against the rivet, then CAREFULLY turn it a little more, so it spreads the link plates a hair or two. That should be enough to loosen them from the roller, but not enough to pop the plates off the rivet. When the link is loose, lubricate it and the rest of the chain, so you don't have to deal with other tight links.

C R M You have to ***remove a link*** if all your efforts fail to loosen it up, or if it is really damaged badly, or if you want to shorten the chain to get rid of looseness. Just put the link you want to remove in the driving-out slot, as shown in Illustration 10-4, then screw (cl) the point of the tool in until it drives the rivet out. Make sure the point is butted up square on the end of the rivet as you drive it out.

C R M Drive the thing until the end of the rivet that is *far-thest* from the point of the tool is almost flush with the outer edge of the casing of the chain tool, then *stop!* Don't drive the rivet all the way out of the chain or you'll never get it back in. Back (c-cl) the point of the chain tool all the way out of the hole in the chain. Take the chain out of the slot in the tool. Does the chain come apart? If not, hold the chain on either side of the driven-out rivet so it is pointing away from you. Then curve both sides of the chain toward you so that the plates spread a bit and release the driven-out

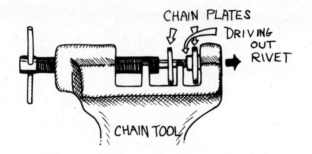

10-4 Chain Tool Driving Out Rivet

rivet. Don't bend the chain hard or you'll misshape the plates. Drive out another rivet so you remove one or more complete links, and wind up with two chain ends that can fit back together.

C R M Stick these ends together and drive the rivet home. To do this you have to put the link in the driving slot of the tool, as shown in Illustration 10-4, but with the point of the tool backed (c-cl) way out to make room for that protruding rivet. Drive the rivet all the way in, until the ends are flush with the outer sides of the sideplates. This takes a gentle touch. If the newly driven rivet is tight, try to loosen it by using the methods described at the beginning of this *tight or bent links* section.

C R M *Chain worn, or lots of kerchunking.* Your chain has seen a lot of hard service, and maybe you replaced the rear sprockets but not the chain. The chain is probably so worn and stretched that it won't fit onto the sprocket teeth properly, so it jumps and kerchunks every time you pedal hard, especially in high gears. To make sure it is a worn chain causing the trouble, just pull forward on one of the links that are wrapped around the front of the chainring, as shown in Illustration 10-5. If the chain pulls away from the chainring until you can see some of the tips of the teeth under it, your chain is worn out and ready for replacement. Lubricate the chain if it is dry, and take it easy as you ride home. Then get a replacement chain and put it on, as described below.

C *Chain replacement.* On cruisers, start by turning your bike upside down. Then find a U-shaped or wide plate on one of the links (called the master link). Pry that plate off (see Illustration 10-1).

M R On derailleur bikes, take the chain tool and put a link in the driving slot (the one farthest from the twist handle—see Illustration 10-4). Screw (cl) the driving point in until it hits one of the chain rivets. Make sure the point is butted up square on the end of the rivet. Drive (cl) the rivet out until the end that's *farthest* from the driving point is just flush with the outer edge of the casing of the chain tool, then *stop!* Don't drive the rivet all the way out of the chain. (See Illustration 10-2.) Back (c-cl) the point of the chain tool all the way out of the hole in the chain. Take the chain out of the slot in the tool. Does the chain come apart? If not, hold the chain on either side of the driven-out rivet. The rivet is pointing away from you. Now bend both sides of the chain toward you so that the plates spread a bit and release the driven-out rivet. Don't bend the chain hard—you'll just misshape the plates. Take the chain off the bike; go to a

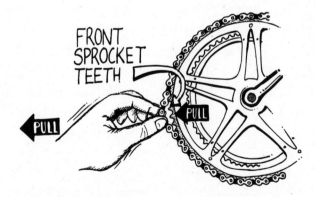

10-5 Checking Chain Looseness

good shop and get as high quality an exact replacement as you can afford.

C It's a lot easier to put the new chain together if you loosen (c-cl) the rear axle nuts and slip the rear wheel forward a bit. Put the chain around the front and rear sprockets and pinch the master link on with pliers. Pull the wheel back in the drop-outs so the chain is tight, then realign the wheel, and tighten the big nuts.

M R For derailleur bikes, you have to make sure you're getting the same width chain as your old one. Get a longer chain and shorten it to the number of links of your old chain. One end of the new chain will be the narrow link with the roller between the ends of the plates. The other end will have two widely spaced plates with no roller between them. (See Illustration 10-2.) Remove the extra links of chain from the end with the widely spaced plates with no roller between them. Drive out the rivet of a link that will create a matching end. Put the chain on the bike. Make sure it traces that backward "S" through the changer rollers, so they pull it tight. Stick the two ends of the chain together, and drive the rivet home (until equal ends stick out of the side-plates) to complete the new chain. Make sure you have the chain on the bike correctly before you drive in the connecting rivet.

M R If you have to drive a new rivet to replace your chain, check the link that you have just re-riveted. It often gets tightened up in the rivet-driving process. To loosen it, see *tight link* above. If you replaced your chain because it was old and worn out, you often have to replace the rear sprockets. They wear down too, and a new chain won't fit them. See rear sprocket PROBLEMS on page 180.

CHAPTER 11

Back Half of Power Train and Gear Changers

Rear Sprockets

DESCRIPTION: C R M It's the little metal wheel with the points on it for the chain, which is attached to the right side of the rear wheel. For cruiser people, this part is so obvious and trouble-free that I hardly need mention it. For multi-speed bike people, however, there can be five, six, seven, eight, or nine rear sprockets or cogs, all attached as a cluster to either a freewheel that is screwed onto the hub of the wheel, or a cassette, which is screwed into the hub. The freewheel or cassette has a ratchet inside, which is why the bike doesn't go backward when you pedal backward; it's also why you can coast downhill. The sprockets on the freewheel or cassette vary widely in size, and therefore in number of teeth. The larger a rear sprocket is, the more teeth it has, and the lower it makes the gear. The front sprockets are just the reverse. Say to yourself a few times, "Front larger higher, rear larger lower," to get it memorized.

PROBLEMS: C R M *Kerchunk*. Your chain kicks up about twice for every revolution of the pedals. The chain jerks annoyingly if you're pedaling hard. Check first to make sure the kerchunk isn't due to a faulty chain or chainring. See the PROBLEMS sections for those parts to fix them. Then check to see if weeds or twigs have wrapped around the freewheel or cassette. If you find debris clogging your sprockets, pull it out or use a screwdriver turned edgewise to scrape between the sprockets as you turn the pedals forward.

M R If the sprockets are clear of debris but still cause the chain to kerchunk, look for worn-down, chipped, or bent teeth on the sprockets. Look closely at the "U" shape between adjacent teeth. If the chain jumps on a given sprocket, especially one of the smallest sprockets, it may well be that the spaces between the teeth are worn-in wider (the teeth are worn narrower, in other words) than those on the other sprockets. You may want to have an ace mechanic check out the sprocket teeth—some modern sprocket and chainwheel teeth are made with uneven edges, so they look chipped or worn down. If your rear sprockets are worn or damaged, all you can do is ride home or to a shop. If you can get chain whips or a freewheel remover for your cassette or freewheel, you can remove those worn sprockets and replace them, as described below.

C If a cruiser rear sprocket is causing the kerchunk, remove the wheel (see *wheel removal* on page 96), pry off the ring-spring that's holding the sprocket, and replace the sprocket with one the same size.

M R *Cassette sprocket (cog) replacement.* Get the bike up on a rack and remove the rear wheel. (See ***wheel removal***.) Unscrew (c-cl) the big axle nut off the right end of the axle or unscrew (c-cl) the quick-release conical nut from the end of the quick-release skewer (if you have a quick release, a spring will come off the axle—don't lose it). Fit your narrow freewheel remover into the splined hole in the lockring that is in the center of the smallest cog. Now either screw (cl) the big axle nut back on the axle, or screw (cl) the quick-release conical nut back onto the skewer, until the nut is snug against the narrow freewheel remover.

M R Now hold the wheel, cogs-down, over a vise, and tighten the jaws of the vise carefully onto the flat sides of the narrow freewheel remover. If you don't have a vise, a big adjustable wrench will do if you use it carefully. Then take a chain whip and put it on the innermost (largest) cog so you can pull clockwise on it, as shown in Illustration 11-1. Use the chain whip and vise or big wrench to loosen the lockring, a bit at a time. The minute you feel the lockring come loose, take the big wrench or vise jaws off that narrow freewheel remover, and spin the lockring off the rest of the way with your fingers, so you don't mess up its threads. When it comes off, remove it and all the sprockets and spacers under it and place them carefully in a row on a clean rag. Keep them in the order they came off. This is very important, because the spacers as well as the cogs vary in size and thickness. Get exact replacements for the cog or cogs that were worn or damaged. This is no small feat. Cogs for 5, 6, 7, and 8-gear cassettes of the same brand can be different, and there are custom, easy-shifting cogs of a mind-boggling array of designs. But don't take a similar substitute for your original. They often don't thread on right, or don't work with indexed shifters, or don't work at all. When you have your exact replacement, put it and all the other parts back onto the cassette in the correct order, then screw

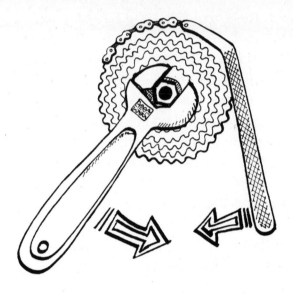

11-1 Chain Whip and Remover in Action

on (cl) the lockring, tightening it carefully with your big wrench or vise on the freewheel remover.

Ⓜ Ⓡ *Freewheel removal and replacement.* (Note: this procedure does NOT apply to cassettes; if your whole cassette needs replacement, have a shop do it with their special tools.) Get the bike up on a rack and remove the rear wheel. (See ***wheel removal*** on page 96.) Unscrew (c-cl) the big-axle nut or quick-release conical nut off the right end of the axle. (If you have a quick release, a spring will come off the axle—don't lose it.) Put whichever you have in a jar where you won't lose it. See if your freewheel remover will fit into place on the freewheel around the axle. If it won't—even though you're sure it's the right size—the spacer nut on the axle is in the way. Get a thin spanner and put it on the *left* cone. Get another spanner or a wrench on the spacer nut (the end of the spacer nut is hex-shaped, just like a thin locknut), loosen (c-cl) it, and unscrew it all the way off the axle. Put it in the jar.

SLOTS FOR REMOVER

11-2 Freewheel with Slots

M **R** Now put the remover in place so that either the splines are well engaged, or the two prongs are set *all* the way down in their slots on the freewheel. (See Illustration 11-2.) Put the big axle nut, or the conical quick-release nut (without its spring) back on the axle and thread (c-cl) it on until it's hand-tight. Take a big wrench and get a good grip on the remover.

M **R** To loosen the freewheel is often very difficult, especially if the wheel and freewheel have been together for a long time or you are a strong rider. Make sure you are turning the remover correctly (c-cl). Also make sure that the big-axle nut or the quick-release conical nut is holding the remover snug against the freewheel. Turn the wrench harder and harder. If you feel something give, check to make sure the freewheel is coming loose and not stripping (sometimes, with the pronged remover, the "give" is from the remover gouging into the freewheel). If the freewheel comes loose, loosen (cl) the big-axle nut or the quick-release conical nut and spin (c-cl) the freewheel off the hub. If the freewheel starts to strip, don't try to get it off—you'll just strip it more. Take off the remover and take the wheel to a shop. They will hopefully be able to get the thing off.

M R When you have spun the freewheel all the way off, you may find one or two little spacer rings underneath it. Save these and put them under the new freewheel. You may have a big, wide, metal or plastic plate under the free-wheel, too. This is a spoke protector, which is meant to keep the chain from running into the spokes if your derailleur gets out of adjustment. If you don't trust your ability to keep the gears tuned up, you can keep the protector on there.

M R Get a good new freewheel to replace your old one if you can. Splurge a little. It makes a difference in the smoothness of the gear operation, and a good freewheel will last longer, too. Whenever you change a freewheel, you usually have to change your chain, especially if the chain is old. Old, stretched chains tend to kick up on new sprockets. You should match the sprockets of the new freewheel with those of the old one. If you want to change to a freewheel with a bigger large rear sprocket, you will have to get more chain. This, in turn, will often tax the tension roller on your changer beyond its capabilities. You will have to change the entire changer system, just to get a slightly lower gear. Changing from a 5 to a 6, 7, 8, or 9-sprocket freewheel can also cause all kinds of problems.

M R Put some Never-seez or similar thread compound on the threads of the new freewheel, then hold the freewheel in one hand, and the wheel (with the spacers on it) in the other, and get ready to start threading the freewheel on. *Careful:* The aluminum alloy used for many hubs is soft. To make sure you get a good start, hold the center section of the freewheel against the axle with a finger and twist counterclockwise, keeping the freewheel exactly vertical, until you feel the threads join. Then twist gently clockwise. Stop immediately if there is any resistance, back the freewheel off (c-cl), using the remover if necessary, and try again. Persevere. When the freewheel finally spins on, it's gratifying. You don't have to tighten up the freewheel. You will do that automatically as you pedal. Put the spacer back on the axle if you had it off, and the big-axle nut or the quick-release conical nut and its spring. Put the wheel back in the frame, hook up your new chain (see ***chain replacement***), and you're set to go. After you've ridden the bike a little, tightening the freewheel on well by your pedaling, check the rear changer adjustment, as described on page 188.

Gear Changers

DESCRIPTION: Ⓜ Ⓡ The changers are the devices for shifting the gears on a bike.

Ⓜ Ⓡ The most common kind of changer is the derailleur type, which moves the chain from larger to smaller sprockets, thus increasing or decreasing the gear ratio. This type of system offers a wide range of gears, transmits a very high percentage of your energy to the rear wheel, and is comparatively easy to repair because of its accessibility. The only drawback is that the derailleur system requires some attention now and then, and you have to use it carefully because of its unprotected location. Don't lay the bike down on its right side, for a start. And don't bump the rear changer, or hit it with anything.

DIAGNOSIS: Ⓜ Ⓡ As with brakes, gear changer systems are made up of three units: the lever, the cable, and the changer or derailleur mechanism itself. Different problems are liable to be caused by each of the different units, but many common problems require that you treat the whole changer system as a whole. Test the gear system for each of the following problems, then follow the procedure indicated.

PROBLEMS: Ⓜ Ⓡ If your gears are *shifting roughly,* or *not going into gear* when you shift, and you have an indexed (click-shifter) system, first try a little *indexed system fine-tuning,* as described on page 194. If that doesn't help, do the full *changer system adjustment* procedure in this section. If you are new to multispeed bikes and have all kinds of little problems shifting, see the *gear changing hints* section in this chapter.

Ⓜ Ⓡ If you have *gear slippage,* particularly a tendency of the chain to slip from a large sprocket to a smaller one, either front or rear, then you are probably using a friction control lever, and the lever is probably loose. Tighten the pivot bolt of your gear lever; it's the bolt the lever pivots around, and there is usually a way to adjust how tight it holds the lever still after you move it.

Ⓜ Ⓡ If your *chain is throwing,* find out if it throws off a front or a rear sprocket, then do the part of the *changer system adjustment* that applies to that half of the system, then see Front Changer PROBLEMS or Rear Changer PROBLEMS. Two hints can save you from many chain throwing problems: *Don't ever drop or put your bike down on its tender right side, and don't ever backpedal while shifting the gears!*

Ⓜ Ⓡ If your *chain rubs the front changer* all the time, first fiddle a bit with the lever for the front changer and see if you can move the cage enough to clear the chain. If that doesn't help, see *rubbing* on page 206. If grindy noises persist even when the front changer is adjusted, see Front Sprocket PROBLEMS.

Ⓜ Ⓡ *Gear changing hints.* If you do all the mechanical adjustments above and still have a grindy or jumpy gear system, the problem may be in the way you are trying to use the gears. You may be trying to force them to shift when you're pedaling hard, or you may be trying to shift them too slowly, or you may simply be using a combination of sprockets that your bike isn't up to using.

M R If you are new to riding a multispeed bike, take an hour or two to practice the art of shifting through all those gears. If possible, get the bike up on a rack (see page 96 for hints) and practice with the rear wheel off the ground; you can have a friend rotate the pedals while you work the gear levers. Or just ride around in a big empty parking lot, one with no islands, lamp posts, or other obstacles, and go through all the gears, looking down at the chain and sprockets as you go. Remember to take all pressure off the pedals, but still keep them rotating, every single time you shift gears. Practice until you can shift quickly, crisply, and accurately into and out of all the usable gears.

M R It takes a quick, decisive flick of the gear lever or grip shift to make the changer lift and move the chain smoothly and quickly from one sprocket to another. Once you get the feel of that decisive flick, all future gear shifting will be easier. Just make sure, when you shift gears down as you go up a hill, that you remember to take all your pressure off the pedals at the moment you shift gears.

M R Remember, too, as you learn, that there are a couple of gears you can't use. On many bikes, it isn't easy for the chain to run from the biggest front sprocket (chainring) to the biggest rear sprocket, or from the smallest front sprocket to the smallest rear sprocket. The chain runs at too sharp an angle; it is either stretched very tight or sagging very loose. It's a strain on the whole system, and it lets you know by making unhappy noises and jumping off the sprockets. Now, in a jam, anybody can make the oversight of shifting into one of those gear combinations. We all do it now and then. But the point is that you should shift out of those extreme sprocket combinations as soon as you can; the

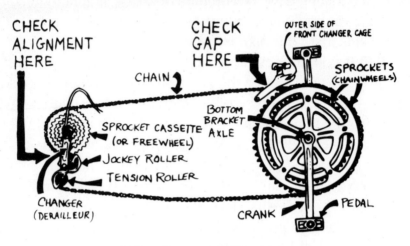

11-3 Changer Adjustment

gears achieved by those combinations can be matched, more or less, by other combinations of sprockets, anyway.

M R *Changer system adjustment.* OK. This is the procedure to follow if your gears aren't working smoothly, and you have already tried a little fine-tuning (page 194), and you have learned how to shift gears smoothly, as described in the *gear changing hints* section, above.

NOTE: M R On many indexed gear systems, if you have shifting problems, you have to run through ALL of the following procedures to catch the cause of the problem, or to correct a combination of causes. So don't try to randomly fiddle with parts of the gear system; follow this procedure in the order presented, and you'll be sure to lick your problem before you're through.

M R The procedure involves putting the bike in the highest gear and adjusting both front and back changers, then putting the bike in its lowest gear and adjusting the changers again. Adjusting the whole gear system is no small feat. Don't cut corners. At least check each adjustment as you go through the steps. If you aren't familiar with the names of the different parts of your changer system, look at Illustration 11-3 to get an overview. Then look at the changer and control-lever illustrations later in this chapter. When you know stuff like where the cable anchor bolts are on your changers, and what the range screws are, then start the adjustment procedure.

M R If your system is made up of a mixed set of parts, like a lever or grip-shift unit made by one company and a changer made by someone else, it is unlikely that you will be able to get things running smoothly. You'll probably just have to find one gear that works and limp home, then go to a shop and get parts that are all of the same type, or certifiably interchangeable. It is a crying shame that there is so little standardization in gear systems, but that is the situation, and crying won't fix it. If we, as consumers, can find certifiably interchangeable parts, we should buy them. That is the only way we can discourage this incompatible-component crap.

M R To start your changer system adjustment, get the bike up off the ground, or at least have a friend hold the rear wheel up off the ground. If you are adjusting an indexed system, set the control lever to *friction* mode. There's usually a little mark for friction mode, and a way to switch into it (push a little button or twist the round cap of the lever unit). You'll know you're in friction mode when you can move the control lever and not hear any clicks. Some systems, especially under-the-bar push-button ones, don't allow you to switch into friction mode. This is a pain, but the procedure is still the same otherwise; you just have to put up with the clicks and some uneven gears until things are adjusted.

M R Turn the pedals forward and shift the bike into its highest gear. That means the gear where the chain runs on the largest front sprocket (chainring) and the smallest rear sprocket (cog). If the chain throws off either sprocket, feed it back on by hand and move the control lever a bit if you have to in order to make it stay there.

■M ■R If you are able to get the chain to stay on the largest front and smallest rear sprocket, skip the next paragraph and get on with the adjustment.

■M ■R If your changers cannot put the chain onto the highest gear sprockets, the cables might be too tight or loose. If the front-changer cable is too loose, so you can pull the lever all you want and it won't push the chain onto the big sprocket, push the lever the other way, so the chain goes onto the smallest front sprocket, then loosen (c-cl) the cable anchor bolt on the front changer, pull the end of the cable until there is just a smidgen of slack left, then tighten (cl) the anchor bolt and shift that baby into high gear, so the chain is on the biggest front sprocket, where you wanted it.

■M ■R If the rear changer is unable to shift the chain onto the smallest sprocket, first turn the adjusting sleeve all the way in (cl) and back it out (c-cl) about two turns. If that doesn't help, loosen (c-cl) the cable anchor bolt and loosen the cable a bit, so the changer can shift the chain onto that smallest sprocket. Tighten (cl) the cable anchor bolt, leaving NO extra slack. OK, you should now have the chain running on the biggest front sprocket and the smallest rear one. What's that? You STILL can't get into the highest gear, even with the cable tension adjusted? The changers need range adjustment. Read on; that's the next step.

■M ■R To ***adjust the changers in highest gear,*** start with the front one and get it aligned, then adjusted. Look down on the changer cage from above. What you should see, when you're in that high gear position, is the outer side of the changer cage aligned so that its central portion is parallel with the big chainring, and adjusted so the outer sideplate of the cage is just missing the outer side of the chain.

[M] [R] First make sure the cage is lined up parallel to the chainring. Look down on the changer and shift it to a lower gear. With the chain off that big sprocket, you should be able to eyeball the plane of the outer side of the changer cage and the plane of the chainring, and see if they are parallel. If the changer is mounted askew on the seat tube, so the front end of that outer side of the cage either aims toward the bike or away from it, the changer won't work right. Sometimes the forward end of the side of the cage is purposely tweaked in a little, and sometimes there may be a jog in the cage shape near the back end of it, but that's not what concerns you. The central part of the cage, nearest to the mounting bridge thingie that holds it to the rest of the changer—*that's* the part that has to be parallel to the chainring. (See Illustration 11-12.) If that section isn't parallel to the chainring, shift the front changer into the lowest gear (smallest sprocket) and loosen (c-cl) the mounting bolt that holds the whole changer to the bike frame.

[M] [R] Twist the whole changer back and forth a little bit at a time, until the outer cage is lined up in a parallel plane with the big chainring. Make sure the changer doesn't slip up or down the frame tube; that outer cage needs to be set so it clears the big chainring by about ⅛ inch or so, as well as being in a parallel plane. When the cage is lined up right, and at the right height still, tighten (cl) the changer mounting bolt firmly.

[M] [R] Once you have aligned the front changer, put it back in high gear, so the chain is on the biggest chainring, and check for a little clearance between the outer side of the chain and the outer side of the changer cage. See Illustration 11-3 for where the gap is. There should be a gap of about ¹⁄₁₆ inch, or the width of a standard pencil lead. Not much, in other words. If the gap is too big, tighten (cl) the high-range screw on the front changer. If the outer side of the cage is hitting the chain, or if you couldn't even get the changer to push the chain up onto the biggest chainring, loosen (cl) the high-range screw. The high-range screw is usually the one that's farthest from the seat tube. Use a small screwdriver to adjust it.

M R The surest way to get the adjustment right is to loosen (c-cl) the screw enough so you can move the changer with the control lever to get that ¹⁄₁₆-inch gap between the cage and the chain, then tighten (cl) the high-range screw until you see or feel the end of the screw touch the body of the changer. On good changers you can look right in there and see the point of the screw. After turning it in until it touches, back off (c-cl) the screw a quarter turn or less. That should adjust the high range perfectly.

M R To adjust the rear-changer high range, kneel or sit down behind the bike, on the right side, and look forward at the changer. It should be feeding the chain up onto the smallest rear sprocket. Find the high-range screw. (It's usually marked with an H.) If the screw head isn't marked, or if the H is so small and covered with grut you can't see it, you have to peer inside the changer body and figure out which of the two range screws has its tip closest to touching the corresponding nub on the changer body. The tip of the low-range screw should be far away from its nub. The tip of the high-range screw may even be hidden by the nub it is touching or almost touching. At any rate, when you locate the high-range screw, turn it in (cl) until the tip touches the nub on the changer body, then back it off (c-cl) about a half turn.

M R Now look at the changer from the back of the bike and see if the chain is feeding straight up from the jockey roller of the changer onto the smallest rear sprocket. If you have something straight, like a pump, you can line it up with the smallest sprocket, as the ruler is lined up in Illustration 11-4. If the changer is out too far, or not out far enough, adjust the high range screw until things are lined up right. If the rollers are out of line, so the chain has to bend to go onto the smallest sprocket, you need to align the changer or the back end of your frame. You can try to do this by putting an Allen key in the pivot bolt for the changer (the bolt that holds the whole thing to the drop-out) and levering either up or down on the Allen key, but this rarely gives you enough leverage to get things aligned. If you are unable to align the rear changer, just adjust it as well as you can, ride home, then take the bike to a first-rate shop and see if they can do it with their special tools and techniques. Sometimes you have to just replace the changer, if it is so bent it won't align properly.

RULER
IN LINE
WITH SMALL
SPROCKET
AND
BOTH ROLLERS

11-4 Rear Changer in High Gear

🅼 🆁 When you have adjusted the changers as well as you can in their highest gear, it's time to put the whole system in its lowest gear. That means shifting the chain to the small- est front sprocket and the largest rear sprocket. If the chain throws off either sprocket, feed it back on by hand and adjust the control lever so it stays on. If the chain can't make it onto one of the sprockets, you may have to loosen (c-cl) one of the low range screws a bit, or adjust one of the cables. If the rear changer can't get the chain onto the biggest sprocket even when you pull the lever as far as it'll go, you have to put the changer back in the high gear and tighten the cable. If the front changer won't let the chain go down to the smallest sprocket, you might have to loosen the cable to the front changer. In either case, loosen (c-cl) the anchor bolt, adjust the cable length, and retighten (cl) the anchor bolt.

🅼 🆁 To *adjust both changers' low range,* check the low-range screws. First adjust the one on the front changer so there is a $\frac{1}{16}$-inch gap between the inner side of the chain and the inner side plate of the changer cage. Then go back to the back of the bike and adjust the low-range screw on the rear changer so the chain feeds straight up from the changer rollers onto the biggest rear sprocket. Now run through all the gears and see if they work well.

🅼 🆁 If you have an indexed system, switch the round thingie on the lever from friction into index mode and see if the clicks match the shifts of the changer. If they don't, do a little fine-tuning, as follows.

🅼 🆁 *Indexed system fine-tuning.* If you have aligned and adjusted your indexed system as explained above, you still may have a bit of rough shifting. Make sure the system is in its indexed mode, then put the front changer in the highest gear, and the rear changer in the second highest gear if its a Shimano system, or the highest gear (smallest rear sprocket) if its a Sun Tour or other system. Crank the pedals around with one hand, and turn the adjusting sleeve at the rear changer counterclockwise until you just begin to hear the chain pinging against the next lower (larger) sprocket, like it wants to shift onto that sprocket. Then turn

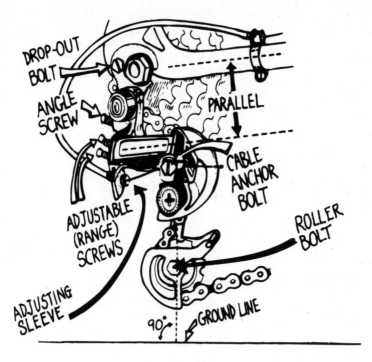

11-5 Rear Changer

the adjusting sleeve back in (cl) about a quarter turn or so. Try shifting through all the gears. It may take a quarter turn, more or less, to zero in on the optimum cable tension for your system.

M R If you have trouble shifting the rear changer into lower gears, you may have to adjust the angle of the dangle of the changer. Try turning the angle screw in (cl) a turn or two. This should pivot the changer down and back, so there's more room between the jockey roller and those large rear sprockets. Just don't turn that screw in too far; the changer body is supposed to be roughly horizontal, and the jockey roller should always be within ¼ inch of the rear sprocket teeth.

M R If shifting is still rough after fine-tuning, there must be some problem other than adjustment. Check all of the following possibilities: Make sure the cables are held firmly in the anchor bolts; that's a common cause of recurrent gear problems. The cable may also be sticky and gunked up with mud or grit; clean and lubricate it. The cable housing may be kinked; straighten the kink with your hands. The cable may be old and frayed; check near the ends for this problem. If you find frayed cable, get the system in a middle gear that's usable and don't shift it again, all the way home. Then replace the cable, as described on page 204.

M R The changer may be clogged with mud or rust; clean and oil the joints. Your control lever may be loose or damaged; tighten the pivot bolt on it if you can, or limp home and get a replacement for the whole lever unit (they used to make levers you could work on, but alas, those days are gone). The front or rear sprockets may be bent, chipped, or worn down; see Front Sprocket and Rear Sprocket PROBLEMS. The chain may be loose or shot; see Chain PROBLEMS. If the bike has been in a bad wreck and the frame is bent, or if the rear wheel or the front half of the drive train has been replaced, the chain line may be off. There's nothing you can do about this out in the backcountry. Just find a gear that works and ride home in it, then take the bike to a real top-notch shop that can take on a complex problem like a messed-up chain line.

Control Lever or Grip

DESCRIPTION: M R There are four different types of levers, and both friction and indexed models of each type. And there are gear controls that are built into the handlebar grips.

M First, the levers. There is a thumb trigger (see Illustration 11-6), which is mounted on the top of the handlebar. They often have settings for indexed and friction shifting. Many also have some sort of position setting; if you loosen the screw that holds the lever down, you can shift the whole thing clockwise or counterclockwise so your thumb can reach it easily.

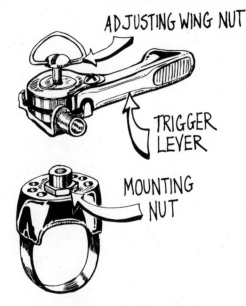

ADJUSTING WING NUT

TRIGGER LEVER

MOUNTING NUT

11-6　Thumb Trigger

Ⓜ Another type of lever is the double type. The levers are placed under the handlebars. You press one of the two levers to shift up, and pull the other to shift down. On some systems, you have to press or pull a lever for each shift (most often when shifting from a low gear to a high gear on the rear changer, or from a high gear to a low gear on the front changer); other systems let you shift through several gears at once.

Ⓡ A third type of control lever fits in the end of the handlebar. It is known as a bar end shifter (see Illustration 11-8). It is held in the bar by an expander bolt that tightens (c-cl) and loosens (cl). The head of this bolt is hidden under the lever, though, so you have to take the lever off to get at it.

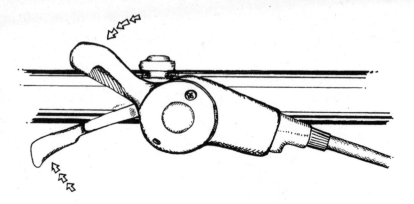

11-7 Double Control Lever

R Most road bikes have gear control levers that are integrated into the brake levers. On most models, you move the brake lever to one side to shift to a larger chainring or cog, and you click a smaller, sub-lever the same way to shift to a smaller chainring or cog. In basic design and function, these are much like the double-type control levers that mountain bikes have under the handlebars. See the indexed system procedures for repairs.

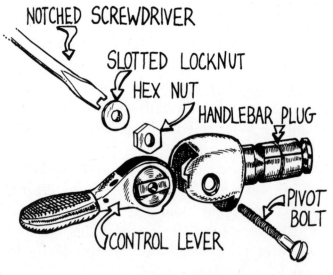

11-8 Tip (Bar End) Shifter

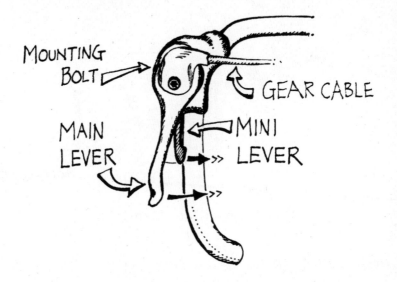

MOUNTING BOLT

GEAR CABLE

MAIN LEVER

MINI LEVER

11-9 Brake Lever Gear Control

🆁 On some old road bikes, there are down-tube type control levers (see Illustration 11-10), which are usually attached to bosses (mounting bumps) on the down tube of the bike frame. All down-tube shifters have long levers that are held in place by wire wing screws or screws. They have many little parts arranged around the pivotal screw. On friction system control levers, the wire wing screw can be adjusted while you ride. If your gears slip a little, you just tighten up the wire thing a bit, and continue happily on your way. Indexed systems have even more little parts around the pivot screws. They usually have two settings, one for indexed shifting and one for friction.

🅼 In addition to these control levers, there are gear controls built into the handlebar grip, such as the Grip Shift (see Illustration 11-11). These have no lever at all. To change gears, you simply twist the inner portion of each handlebar grip, and the gears change. You'll hear a click or (if you are shifting the front changer) several clicks as you switch from one gear to another.

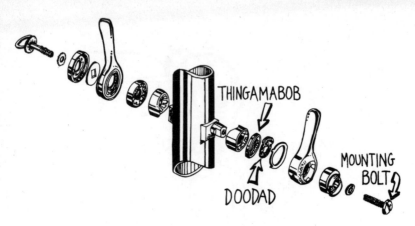

11-10   Down-Tube Control Lever

PROBLEMS: Ⓜ Ⓡ *Stickies, indexed system levers.* If you have stickies or rough operation of an indexed system control lever, you usually have to replace the whole lever. Unscrew (c-cl) the mounting bolt that holds the lever to the bike or to the mounting bracket (on many mountain bike levers, the head of this bolt is behind the bracket), take the lever off the bike (see page 36 if you need to take the handlebar grip and brake hand lever off to do this), undo

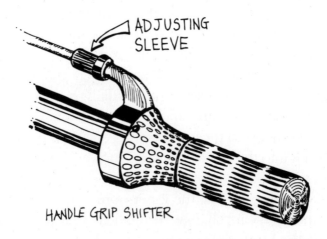

11-11   Grip Shift

the cable and pull it out, then take the lever to a good shop for an exact replacement. Thread the cable back into the new lever, place the lever (setting it in the comfortable finger position if it's a thumb trigger), then tighten (cl) the mounting bolt. This procedure is relatively simple on most thumb triggers and double-lever units, but it can be quite tricky on down-tube control levers for indexed systems. The mounting bolt holds a lot of little doodads and specially shaped thingamabobs, often different ones on the left and right levers. Arrgh.

M *Stickies, grip control.* If your grip control is hard to move or won't stay put in a gear, you probably have mud, rust, or broken parts somewhere in the works. Try squirting a little oil on the cable right where it goes into the body of the control; work the grip back and forth to see if things loosen up. No go? You may need to replace a cable, which is a tricky operation best left to bike-shop mechanics, unless you have lots of time, patience, and high aptitude for 3-D games.

M If it's clear that the grip is clogged with mud or broken inside, you can loosen the Allen bolt that binds the control unit to your handlebars, then slide the bar grip (and bar ends, if you have them) off the handlebars, then slide off the gear control unit, loosen the cable anchor bolt at the changer mechanism, pull the cable off the bike, then take the cable and control unit to a shop for replacement. Slide the new control unit on the handlebar, then tighten (cl) the Allen bolt to hold it in place so the cable housing aims down like the one on the other end of the handlebar. Put your handlebar grip end back on, and your bar end, if you have one of those. Put the grip control in its loosest position (with the cable extended fully). Thread the cable back into place and tighten (cl) the anchor bolt on the changer. Try out the gears. If they need adjustment, see the ***indexed system fine tuning*** section earlier in this chapter.

◫ If you have to replace a down-tube control lever for an indexed system, either have a shop do it, or get the installation instructions for your specific lever, and follow them to a "T." If the instructions are written in about six different languages and the English is a little unclear, just take a look at the German version. Whew! They sure use big words, don't they? And with unreal numbers of consonants all in a row. They tell you about things like "Umschalten auf Reibungsschalten." This makes it clearer that we shouldn't feel too bad about the slightly unclear English version. At any rate, when you are done mounting your new gear lever and need to get the cable reset, see the ***cable replacement*** procedure, below.

◫ ***Stickies, bar-end lever.*** If you have a bar-end type shifter that needs replacing, take a big old screwdriver and file a notch in the end, then loosen (c-cl) and remove the slotted nut first, then unscrew (c-cl) the pivot bolt and pull the lever out for replacement. When reassembling, slide the lever in so the square bump fits into the square slot, then put the hex-nut in its hex-hole and screw the pivot bolt in (cl) until it is snug. This adjustable pivot bolt also serves as the tension bolt, like the wing bolt on the other levers. Tighten it (cl) until the lever works smoothly but with resistance, then tighten (cl) the slotted nut with the notched screwdriver.

◫ ***Slippage or stickies on a friction system lever***. On a friction system, either your lever is very easy to move back and forth, and moves by itself, allowing the gears to shift, or your lever is hard to move, and then moves by itself after you shift. *Don't* oil the control lever. Usually, the problem with a slipping or sticky friction system control lever is the adjustment of the wing bolt or screw. If the lever is slipping, tighten (cl) the wing bolt. If the lever is so tight that you have trouble shifting smoothly, loosen (c-cl) the wing bolt a wee bit. You tip-shifter people, loosen the slotted locknut, then tighten (cl) or loosen (c-cl) the pivot bolt, then retighten (cl) the locknut.

R If the stickiness persists, you may have a dirty unit. To clean it, you have to take it apart by unscrewing (c-cl) the adjustable bolt. Watch it! There may be quite a few little hard-to-distinguish parts held together by that bolt. As the bolt comes out, try to hold things together with your fingers and take them apart one piece at a time, memorizing the order of things as you go. The sample I have illustrated is typical, but there are many variations. Get the order of your parts straight. If parts spew all over when you take the adjustable bolt off, look at an identical lever, like the other one on your bike if you have two. Clean all the rubbing surfaces with a clean dry rag. Use fine steel wool on the metal parts if you have to. If any of the parts is badly rusted or bent, take it to a good shop and get an exact replacement. When reconstructing things, check again to make *sure* they are in the right order. Also, make sure any washer with an ear or "dog" on it (if there is one) goes on so the ear fits in its slot. (See Illustration 11-10.) Tighten (cl) or loosen (c-cl) the bolt so that the lever can turn smoothly, but not loosely. Are you still getting slippage? Go on to the cable section.

Cable

DESCRIPTION: M R A thin cable (thinner than a brake cable) that runs from a ball, cylinder, or small barrel end in the control lever or grip control down to the changer mechanism, where it is held in by an anchor bolt. If you have tip, thumb trigger, or grip shifters, there will be some housing around the cable, between the control unit and a housing stop that is bolted onto the down tube of the frame. All rear changer cables run through a short length of housing that curves down from the chainstay to the mechanism. There are different types of housing for different gear systems. Make sure your cable housing is adequate for your system, especially if it is an indexed gear system.

PROBLEMS: Ⓜ Ⓡ *Stickies.* When you shift your control unit, the gears do not change immediately. Or they slip just enough that the chain gets hung up between the two sprockets and spins wildly around and around. Put the lever all the way forward. Look closely at the cable where it comes out of the control lever unit, and where it goes into and comes out of any housing. Is the cable frayed anywhere? Replace it if it's frayed at all. Gear cables have to take a fair amount of strain, and they will fail if you let them get more and more frayed.

Ⓜ Ⓡ *To replace a frayed or broken cable,* loosen the anchor bolt on the mechanism and pull the cable out of the housing and the control lever. Get a new cable with the same sort of control lever end. If you have a grip control unit such as a grip shifter, it is not easy at all to get the cable out of the control unit. I recommend you let a shop do the job.

Ⓜ Ⓡ When you get a new cable, don't cut it to size until you have threaded it through the housing and the cable anchor bolt. When the cable is threaded, push the control lever all the way forward (if you have a thumb trigger or triggers, move the lever to the position that leaves the cable *loosest*). If you are working on a front changer cable, move the mechanism to the lowest gear position. You may have an oddball front derailleur that won't stay in low, but rather goes to high by itself; if so, just attach the cable with the fershlugginger thing in high gear. If it's a rear changer cable, move the mechanism (or let it spring itself) to the highest gear position. Tighten (cl) the anchor bolt. Try the gears out, and adjust the adjusting sleeve on the control lever or changer if necessary (see **indexed system fine tuning** on page 194).

 M R If your cable is not broken or frayed, but you find grit, rust, and gunk at the housing ends, or a kink in the housing, loosen the cable anchor bolt on the mechanism as if you were going to remove the cable. Pull on the mechanism end of the cable with one hand, and operate the control lever with the other. Try oil on the cable where it disappears into the housing ends. For a rear changer cable, try holding the mechanism end of the cable with one hand and pulling the open section of cable that runs along the chain stay with the other. Is there stickiness in the rear section of the cable housing? If not, test for stickies in the front section of housing if there is one.

 M R When you find the area of stickiness, check the housing for kinks, grit clogging it up, or burrs in the ends, and check the cable for evidence of wear. Buy new housing and cable as needed. Get braided housing made for your brand of changer if you have an indexed shifter system. Cut the housing to match the length of the old pieces *exactly*. When cutting coiled housing, work the blades of the wire clipper between the coils, then twist as you cut the wire coil off clean. Check for burrs at the ends of the pieces of housing. Any burr pointing out into the air you can file off. But if there are inner burrs, recut the housing. (See Illustration 2-7.) If you have braided housing, you have to snip it off with the diamond-hole kind of cable clippers.

 M R The section of housing where the cable curves under or over the bottom bracket is a common place for grit to gather, especially on mountain bikes. If you have housing there, and a lot of trouble with grit, you can buy a guide that attaches to the bottom bracket. This setup will replace the housing and collect less grit. If the cable binds as it goes through the short piece of housing that passes over the axle of the rear wheel, it may be because this piece of housing is too short or too long. Cut a new piece of housing that can just make the short arch needed to get around the axle without binding on it.

Front Changer

DESCRIPTION: M R The front changer has a metal cage that moves the chain from sprocket to sprocket. The cage is attached to a movable parallelogram gadget like the one in Illustration 11-12. A spring usually pushes the side of the parallelogram so the cage goes to the left or into the low gear position. When you pull the gear lever, the cable pulls at the anchor bolt and moves the cage to the right or into the high gear position. A couple of oddball derailleurs are reversed; the spring pushes to the right, the cable pulls the cage left or into low gear.

PROBLEMS: M R *Rubbing.* The cage of the front changer rubs against one side or the other of the chain and makes a bothersome noise. First try to eliminate the noise with the control lever. Shifting the rear changer sometimes necessitates adjustment of the front one. If you have a friction system, make sure the adjustable bolt on the control lever is tight enough.

M R The chain is still rubbing the front changer, no matter how you set the lever? Get the bike up on a fence post, or get a friend to hold the rear wheel up, and put your head above the front changer. Crank the pedals forward slowly and watch the chain where it passes between the sides of your front changer cage. You may see a wobble in your sprocket every time it goes around. If so, go to Front Sprocket PROBLEMS. If the chain hits because it is running at a very sharp angle from the front to rear sprockets, you

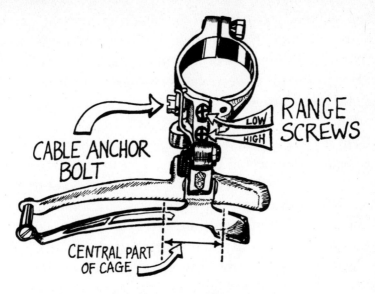

11-12 Front Changer

are using an extreme gear position that isn't practical (see page 188).

[M] [R] The next thing to check out is the alignment and adjustment of the changer. See page 188 for a good procedure to do that. If the changer is aligned correctly on the bike and adjusted properly but the sides of the cage are bent or twisted out of the vertical plane, get out your adjustable wrench and adjust the jaws so they just slip onto the bent side plate. Bend the plate with care and patience, until it is as near to straight and vertical as you can get it; if somebody else you are riding with has a similar front changer, look at theirs to get an idea of how yours is supposed to look.

[M] [R] *Chain throwing, or changer won't shift chain.* When you shift the front changer, it either throws the chain right off the sprockets, or it won't move the chain enough to get it on the largest or smallest sprocket.

[M] [R] First check the alignment and adjustment of the front changer, as described on page 190. If you do that but your chain still tends to throw off the big chainring when you try to shift into it, do this neat trick: Slip your adjustable wrench jaws onto the front tip of the outer side plate of the cage, and bend the tip in very slightly—only ¹⁄₁₆ inch or so. This slightly toed-in cage tip will catch a chain that has throwing tendencies.

M R If your adjusted and aligned front changer can't get the chain *onto* the big chainring, you may be able to slip your adjustable wrench jaws onto the front end of the *inner* side plate of the cage, and tweak it so the bottom edge of the inner plate bends outward (away from the bike) at the front end. Place the jaws of your adjustable wrench at the location indicated by the diagonal dotted line in Illustration 11-12. This is a subtle bend, a sort of twist, and many front changers have bends, lumps, or odd nodules at their front ends that get in your way, but if you can make a little twist at the front edge of the cage, it'll kinda flip the chain upward when you shift, so it goes onto the big chainring more easily. Just don't bend the whole cage out of line in your customizing efforts.

M R If your front changer is adjusted, aligned, and customized nicely at the front end, but the chain *still* throws off—not just when you shift, but also when you go over bumps in the middle of turns and things like that—you might have a very old, loose, or bent chain. See Chain PROBLEMS.

Rear Changer

DESCRIPTION: M R The thing that changes the chain from one rear sprocket to the other. It consists of a changer body and a cage with two chain rollers, one of which holds the chain tight (the tension roller) and one of which moves the chain from sprocket to sprocket (the jockey roller). There are two distinct types of rear changers. One has a box-like body with two closed sides. (See Illustration 11-13.) The range screws may be in different places, and the cable anchor bolt may be easier or harder to get at, but the design is usually very similar.

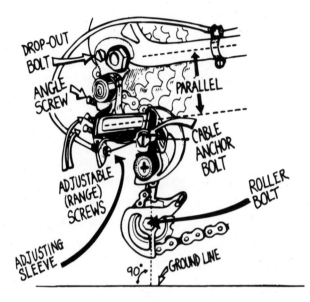

11-13   Rear Changer

PROBLEMS: Ⓜ Ⓡ *Chain throwing.* First make sure the rear changer is aligned and adjusted, as described on page 193. Then make sure it is attached to the frame firmly by its mounting bolt, and not bent. You can straighten some minor bends, like if the arm that holds the tension roller is bent a little, but major bends require that you simply limp home in any gear that works, and replace the whole changer. If the changer is so badly bent that no gears work, see *Changer wrecked,* below.

Ⓜ Ⓡ *Changer wrecked.* Ran over a stick and it got jammed through the chain into the spokes? Whew. That really does a number on the rear changer. Or maybe you just slammed on your right side, and the changer hit a rock. Whatever the reason, the result is the same; you have no gears now. All you can do is take out your chain tool and remove a bunch of links from the chain. The idea is to make it short enough to run from the middle front chainring directly to one of the middle rear sprockets, providing you with one gear and bypassing the broken changer. If any links of the chain got bent or broken in the mishap, make sure you remove those and leave the good links. See Chain PROBLEMS for the procedure used to take links out of the chain.

M R If you can't get the wrecked changer off the bike, at least tie it up to the seat or chain stay to keep it from flapping around and wreaking more havoc in the spokes. When you get home on your one-speed (amazing, isn't it, how well you can get along with just one speed, if you don't hurry) you'll have to get a new changer, and maybe a new chain, if parts of the old chain got twisted in the action.

M R *Changer replacement* is a good alternative to overhaul and alignment, if you can afford it. Any bent changer, or changer with corners and edges knocked off, should be replaced. Start by removing the rear wheel. Then loosen (c-cl) the cable anchor bolt and remove the cable. Unscrew (c-cl) the bolt that holds the changer to the frame drop-out, and take the changer off. Undo (c-cl) one of the roller bolts and remove the roller to release the chain from the roller cage. Take the changer to a good shop and get a new one. Get one that's exactly like your old one, especially if you have an indexed gear system.

M R Tighten (cl) the mounting bolt of your new changer into the drop-out, being careful not to mash the tip of the angle screw against the drop-out tab. If the mounting bolt has a nut that goes on the back of the drop-out, spin the nut on, loosen (c-cl) the mounting pivot bolt about a quarter turn, then hold it still with the Allen key while you tighten (cl) the nut back behind the plate. Take the tension roller (the lower one) out, loop the chain over it, and replace it so that the chain makes a reverse "S" through the rollers. Tighten (cl) the roller bolt up again. If the roller has ball bearings, check to make sure that the roller turns freely without being so loose that it wobbles. Adjust the two cones (cl is tighter, c-cl is looser) as needed. Connect the cable to the cable anchor bolt, and adjust the range-limiting screws so that the changer shifts smoothly into the largest and smallest sprockets without throwing the chain. (See ***Changer System adjustment*** in the Gear Changers section.)

Postscript

I had fun writing this book. I've been riding around in the boonies for over forty years, and I have always loved the great feeling of independence from civilization and closeness to all our relatives out there.

In fact, I think I'll go for a ride right now. If something breaks or gets messed up on my bike that isn't in this book, I'll let you know about it in my next revision.

And if *you* have some problem on a ride, and find out I didn't cover it well enough in this book, I'd sure appreciate it if you'd write the publisher to let me know.

APPENDIX

Vestiges

Anything on a bicycle that isn't essential to its function is vestigial. Extra. Dead weight.

Some extras, which I will list first, can be worth their weight. The others make me feel like I have appendicitis if I write about them, so I refuse to do much more than mention them.

Helmet. **C** **R** **M** A must for all cycling, especially in traffic. There are many high-quality hard-shell and soft-shell helmets. If you shop around, you can find one that's comfortable for you, light, cool, and meets safety standards. There are also bargain helmets and less expensive models made by the major helmet companies. Try these if you are short on cash. But even if you have to spend a bundle to get the helmet that suits you, consider it money well spent—heads are one to a customer.

HELMET
HISTORY

Water bottle. C R M The plastic kind that fits in a little cage that's clamped to the bike frame works fine. In hot places, some people prefer the sack container that straps to your back, with the little hose to your mouth. They make for a hot, sweaty patch on your back, though. On *very* long, dry rides, you may need two or even three water containers. If possible, get containers made out of tasteless food-grade plastic. You can put stuff in the water to replace the electrolytes and salts you lose as you sweat. Just make sure you don't drink large quantities of commercial electrolyte replacers. They can make you sick. I find that the combination of an occasional can of V8, an occasional fruit juice drink, and LOTS of water does the trick. You hate V8? You may need to add a pinch of salt to your water or juice once a day.

Computer. C R M That little oval gizmo that clips to your handlebar and has a digital readout showing your speed and mileage. It's great for racers who want to keep track of their awesome pace, phenomenal distance, record time, and (on some models) whopping heart rate. Humble tourists can also use bike computers to help plan their days and get to lodgings or campsites before dark. I don't like bike

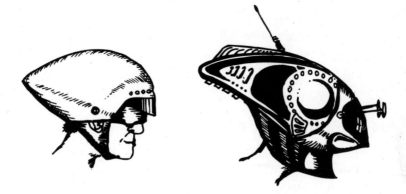

computers, myself. They keep reminding me of how slow I am going. I *know* I'm going slow. I don't need any reminders. If you are looking for a computer for your bike, avoid the ones that require lots of wire and weird stuff attached to the hub of your wheel. The lighter and simpler the thing is, the better.

Light. C R M There are inexpensive ones with batteries, expensive bright ones with batteries, and really high-tech generator ones. The cheap little blinking red tail light works OK for making you visible to motorists. You can clip the basic blinker to the back of your seat post, helmet, or belt. Strap the arm-band model to your leg, not your arm; put it just below the knee so it bobs up and down when you pedal. It looks a bit funny, but it might save your life. You can use one of these in combo with a bright battery-powered headlight, and get along pretty well for rides or commutes in the dark, as long as you only make short trips. I particularly like the headlights that mount on your helmet, with batteries that go in a pack on your back. Get recharge-able batteries and recharge them with a solar charger if you want to be nice to the environment. Most high-tech lights with generators, remote multi-cell battery-packs, multiple multicolored wires, directional signals, toggle switches, and other such vestigial crap are not only unaesthetic—they can be dangerous. The wires can get caught in the works of your bike. Besides, they often don't work after rough usage on the road or soakage in a rain storm. If you find long night rides without a headlight spooky, stick to daytime riding. Simple enough?

Mud guards (fenders). ☑ A useful vestige on city bikes when it's raining. Make sure they are securely bolted at all brace ends. If the braces rub the wheel, loosen (c-cl) the bolts that hold them to the frame and adjust, then retighten (cl) the bolts. That's better than bending the braces out like wishbones. For extra spray protection, glue or tape pie-shaped pieces of plastic sheathing from the drop-outs to the mud guard between the braces. These pieces are most needed at the back of the front wheel and the front of the back wheel. Don't expect them to keep you completely dry, though. Riding in rain is a pain. To reduce the pain in cold weather, put plastic sandwich bags over your socks before you put your shoes on, wear waterproof (neoprene's best) gloves, and put a rubber swimming cap over your head, under your helmet. You'll sweat inside these vapor barriers, but they keep your extremities from wind-chilling, and they can all be washed out and dried easily.

Carrier. ☑ For cycle tourists, Blackburn carriers are unbeatable. They cost a lot, and getting one to fit your bike is sometimes a pain, but they last, which is critical on a long tour. For light-duty use you can get a cheaper carrier that doesn't have to be custom fit to your bike. Carriers go behind the seat, over the rear wheel. Make sure all bolts and nuts for your carrier are kept tight. You can use self-locking "aircraft" or "nylock" nuts; they don't shake loose. You can also get all kinds of fancy racks and bags and panniers for your bike. I don't like having stuff like that on a road or mountain bike. I have a cruiser with a big basket for shopping. When I'm riding for fun on a lightweight bike, I just take a banana or two and my windbreaker in a tiny fanny pack. If I have to carry a little something extra, I use a little cloth rucksack, which I fold up and put into my fanny pack after I've eaten the little something. That rules out camping on a bike for me.

Kickstand. **C** These are useful on around-town bikes. Make sure the bolt (if there is one) that wedges the stand tightly between the chain stays is *extra* tight. If your stand is a little too long for your bike (the bike stands up too straight and falls over easily), try leaning the bike on the stand, then tipping the bike to the left so you lift up the rear wheel three inches. The weight of the bike should now be on the stand. Push down from straight above the stand so that it bends until the rear wheel comes back to earth. Bike leaning over more? It should be. If your crank hits the kickstand now, loosen (c-cl) the bolt that holds the stand, move the stand, and tighten (cl) the bolt well.

Lock. **C** **R** **M** The best lock is the human eye. If you have a high quality, nice-looking bike, take it inside with you, or lock both wheels with a heavy duty "U" type lock to something outside a window that you can keep glancing through. Keep your eye on it. Don't leave a pricey bike locked with *any* lock outside overnight. Agh; I don't like talking about locks. I'll never get over having my dear old Cinelli ripped off. Put it this way. If you steal bikes, please, stop it. If you steal a bike from someone who loves it and depends on it, you are doing one of the lowest things that one human being can do to another.

Chain Guard. **C** Hard to keep from hitting on them with the crank and other things, isn't it? I agree. If yours is troublesome, take it off, and put a rubber band or a pants clip around your cuff.

Other Vestiges:

Brake lever extensions, chain-link jewelry, polycarbonate designer goggles, gold-plated corkscrews, chromed tire-valve caps, "chopper" forks, "sissy" bars, imitation leopard-skin saddle covers. Filth, Filth. Filth and junk. I refuse to say more about them.

Index

A

Abbreviations
  cl; c-cl (clockwise; counter clockwise), viii
  Cruiser; Mountain Bike; Road Bike, viii
Accessories, 215–220
Adjustable wrench, 16
Adjusting
  bearings, 11. *See also specific parts.*
  bottom bracket, 160–161
  brakes, 39–42, 65
  gears, 188–196
  handlebar height, 72
  headset, 78–82
  seat, 137–140
  sleeve, brake, 39, 40, 48
  stem, 72
  wheel hub, coaster brake, 120
"Aircraft" nuts, for carrier, 218
Allen keys (hex keys), 18–19
All-rounder handlebar, 68
Anchor bolt
  brake cable, 38, 46, 47, 48, 52
  gear cable, 188–196, 209
Arms, brake, 46, 48, 52
Ashtabula (one-piece) crank, 154, 162, 163
  bottom bracket of, 163–164
  changing chainring on, 167
  replacing, 163
Axle (spindle)
  bottom bracket, 160
  pedal, 148–152
  wheel hub, 116

B

Back half (power train), 179–211
Balloon tire cruiser, 1, 2
Bearings. *See also specific parts.*
  adjusting, 11
  checking, 15
  greasing, 23
Bent fork, 88
Bent frame, 88–90
Bent handlebars, 73
Bent pedals, 151
Bent rim, wheel, 121
Bent tooth on front sprocket, 165–166
Bent wheel, 121
Binder bolt
  handlebar-stem, 67, 68, 69
  seat, 135, 137
Blackburn carrier, 218
Blip in rim of wheel, 125–127
Bolts and nuts
  for carrier, 218
  checking, 15
  loosening and tightening, 10
Boot, tire, 18, 101
Bottom bracket, 160–164
  adjusting, 160–161
  noises from, 148, 162
  overhaul, 162–164
Brakes, 29–66
  adjusting, 39–42
    coaster, 48, 64–65
    cockeyed shoes, 54–55
    sleeve, 31, 32, 40, 48
  cable, 31, 38. *See also* Cable(s), brake.
  caliper (side-pull), 48
  cantilever, 46
  can't reach, 36
  checking, 15

Brakes, *continued*
    coaster, 30, 58–66
        adjusting, 48, 64–65
        bearing adjustment, 120
        overhauling, 58–66
        wheel removal, 98
        wheel replacement, 109
    description and diagnosis, 29–31
    disk, 29
    dragging, 49–51
    hand lever unit, 31, 32–38
        broken, 36–38
        slippage in, 34–35
        stickies in, 32–34
    loose, 30, 39–42
    mechanism, 31, 46–66
        caliper (side-pull), 48
        cantilever, 46
        coaster, 48, 58–66
        overhaul, 52–54, 58–66
    problems, diagnosis of, 29–31
    shoes (rubber pads), 54–57
        cockeyed, 54–55
        dragging, 49–51
        juddering, 57
        slipping when hot or wet, 55
        squeaking, 57
        stickies, 52
        worn, 55–56
    stickies, 30–31
    units of, 30–31
    V-brake, 46–47
    wheel removal and, 97–98
Broken gear cable, replacing, 204
Broken pedal, 151
Broken spokes, 132–134
Buying a bike, 1–8, 86
Buying tools and parts, 27

C

C (Cruiser)
Cable(s)
    brake, 31, 38–45
        adjusting, 39–42
        broken, 42–45

Cables, *continued*
    carrier, 31, 46
    housing, 43–45
    kink, 44
    replacing, 42–43
    stickies in, 43–45
    cutter, 21–22
    gear, 203–206
        broken, 204
        stickies in, 204–206
    spares, 26
Cage, gear changer, 206, 207
Caliper (side-pull) brakes, 48
Campagnolo hub spanners, 23, 24
Cantilever brakes, 46
Carrier
    brake cable, 31, 46
    eyelets, 5
    luggage, for touring, 218
Cartridge bearings, 11, 116
Chain, 169–178
    checking, 15, 177
    cleaning and oiling, 171–172
    death, 173
    described, 169
    jamming, 169
    kerchunking, 145, 148, 176, 180
    loose, 173
    lubricating, 171–172
    master link, 169, 170, 177
    noise from, 145, 148, 176
    oiling, 171
    replacing, 176–178
    rubbing on gear changer, 206
    spare links, 26
    squeaky or gunky, 171–172
    suckage, 172
    throwing off of sprockets, 169
        from front changer, 207
        from rear changer, 209
    tight link, 174–176
    tool for driving rivets, 19
        driving rivet, 174–176
        spreading link, 174–175
    whip (tool), 25, 181–182
    worn out, 176

Chain guard, 219
Chain lubricant, 23, 171
Chainring, 164–168
  bent tooth, 165
  kerchunk, 164
  wobbles, 167
Chain stay, 85, 157
Chainwheel. *See* Chainring.
Chain whips, 25, 181–182
Changer. *See* Gear changers.
Channel lock pliers, 22–23
Checklist, maintenance, 14–15
cl, c-cl (clockwise and
      counter-clockwise), viii, 10
Clank or clunk, 78, 145, 148
  in bottom bracket, 162
  in cranks, 154
  in headset, 78
  in pedals, 149
Cleaning chain, 171–172
Clipless pedals, loose, 153
Coaster (foot) brake, 29, 58–66
  adjusting, 48, 65–66
  overhauling, 58–66
  wheel bearing adjustment
     with, 120
  wheel removal with, 98
  wheel replacement with, 109
Cockeyed brake shoes, 54
Cog. *See* Rear sprocket (cog).
Comfort, on seat, 140
Control levers (gears), 196–203
Cool Tool, 21
Cottered/cotterless crank. *See* Cranks.
Cotterless crank tool, 26, 158
Cracked stem, replacing, 71–72
Cracking noise in headset, 78
Cranks, 154–159
  adjusting (bottom bracket), 160–161
  Ashtabula (one-piece), 154, 161,
    162
  bent, 157
  clunking or squeaking, 148,
    154–157
  diagnosing noises from, 145, 148

Cranks, *continued*
  loose, 154–157
    Ashtabula, 161, 162
    cotterless, 154–157
  one-piece. *See* Ashtabula.
  overhauling/replacing
    Ashtabula, 162
    cotterless, 158–159
  removing tool, 26, 158
  squeaking, creaking, 148, 154
Crank tool, 26, 154
Creaking noise, 148
Crescent (adjustable) wrench, 16
Crooked stem, 69–71
Crown (fork), 87
Crown race (headset), 84
Cruisers, viii, 1–2. *See all* **C**
    paragraphs.
  Ashtabula crank on, 154, 161, 162
  brakes on, 30, 58–66
  buying, 2
Curb-edge tire test, 111–112
Custom bikes, 6

D

Derailleur. *See* Gear changer.
Dismantling, tips about, 10–11
Double shifters, 197–198
Down tube type shifters, 199–200
Drop bars, 67, 73
Drop-out (frame), 87
Dust cap
  on cotterless crank, 155, 156
  on hub of wheel, 116
  on pedal, 150

E

Edge test (tires), 111–112
Einstein, 4
Epoxy paint, 88
Expander bolt, stem, 69, 71, 72

F

Fenders (mud guards), 218
Ferrule (end sleeve), 38
Flare, in rim, 125
Flat tire, 94–110
Foot brake. *See* Coaster (foot) brake.
Fork, 85–91
    bent, 89
    flutter, 90
    headset and, 81
    shock, squeaky, 90
Fork crown race, 84
Frame, 85–91
    bent, 88–90
    in buying decision, 6, 86
    painting, 86–89
Frayed cable, 42
Freewheel (rear sprockets), 179, 182
Freewheel remover, 25, 182
Front changer, 206–208
    adjusting, 188–195
    aligning, 191
    chain throwing on, 207–208
    rubbing chain, 206
    won't shift, 207–208
Front half (of power train), 147–168
Front sprocket (chainring), 164–168
    bent tooth on, 165
    changing, 166
    kerchunk, 164
    misaligned, 168
    wobbly, 167–168
Front wheel
    removing, 96–97
    replacing, 108

G

Gear changers, 185–211
    adjusting, 188–196
    buying parts for, 189
    cables, 203–206
        broken, 204–205
        stickies, 204, 205

Gear changers, *continued*
    chain rubbing, 206
    checking, 15, 185–186
    control levers, 196–203
    diagnosing problems in, 143–146,
        185–186
    fine-tuning, 194
    front changer, 206–208
        adjusting, 188–195
        aligning, 191
        chain throwing on, 207–208
        rubbing, 206
        won't shift, 207–208
    preventing problems, 186
    rear changer, 208–211
        adjusting, 188–195
        chain throwing on, 209
        noise from, 146
        replacing, 210
        stickies in, 196
    problem diagnosis, 145–146
    roughness in, 186, 188–195
    slippage, 145, 186, 202
    stickies, 196, 204
    troubleshooting, 143–146, 186
Getting a bike. *See* Buying a bike.
Gooseneck. *See* Stem.
Grating noise in bottom bracket, 148,
    162
Graack. *See* Chain, suckage.
Grease and oil, 23
Greasing bearings, 11. *See also specific
    parts.*
Grinding noises
    in bottom bracket, 148, 162
    in headset, 78
Grip. *See* Handlegrips.

H

Hammer, 26
Hand lever unit (brakes), 31, 32–38
Handlebars, 67–76
    drop bar bent in, 73
    loose in stem, 69

Handlebars, *continued*
   replacing, 74
   stem height and, 72
   tape worn or unwound, 74
   too high or low, 72
Handlegrips, removing, 74
Headset, 77–84
   crunchy or grackly, 78
   loose, 78–81
   overhauling, 82–84
   threadless, 77, 79, 81
   tight, 81–82
Head tube, 85
Height of handlebars, 72
Height of seat, 137–139, 140
Helmet, 15, 215
Help, getting it, 13
Hex set screw (Allen) keys, 18–19
Housing, cable, 38, 42–44
Hubs (wheel), 93, 114–121
   loose cones in, 114–120
   overhauling, 58–66, 121
Hub spanners, 23

I

Indexed shifters, 187, 196
Inflating a tire, 111–114

J

Jamming (chain), 169
Joint (of frame), 85

K

Kerchunking of chain, 145, 148, 164,
   176, 180
Knocking noise, crank, 157

L

Lacing, of spokes, 134
Laying down your bike, 219
Leaving your bike, 219
Left and right on the bike, 9
Levers. *See* Control levers (gears),
     Hand lever unit (brakes).
Light, 217
Listening to bike, 12–13
Lock, 219
Looseness. *See also* Slippage.
   in bottom bracket, 160–161
   in brakes, 39–42
   in brake hand levers, 34
   in chain, 173
   in changer control lever, 202
   in crank, 154–157
   of handlebars, 69
   in headset, 78–81
   in pedal, 149
   of seat, 137
   of stem, 69–71
   in wheel, 114–120
Loosening bolts and nuts, 10
Lubricants, 23

M

🅼 (Mountain Bike), viii
Maes handlebars. *See* Drop bars.
Maintenance Checklist, 14–15
Master link, 170, 177
Money, in tool kit, 20
Mountain bike, viii. *See all* 🅼
     paragraphs.
Mud guards (fenders), 218
Mud problems, 43, 196
Multi-tools, 21

N

Never-seez, 159, 184
Nipple, spoke, 121
Noises. *See each type of noise:* clinking,
        cracking, kerchunking,
        knocking, rubbing,
        squeaking.
Nuts, tightening and loosening, 10
"Nylock" nuts, 218

O

Oiling, 23
    bottom bracket, 162
    chain, 15, 171
One brake shoe dragging, 49–51
One-speed bikes. *See* Cruisers.

P

Painting frame, 86–88
Patch kit, 17, 103–106
Pedals, 148–154
    bent, broken, stripped, 151
    clipless, loose, 153
    diagnosing noises from, 145, 148
    loose, tight, or noisy, 149
    replacing, 151
    spanner, 23
Penetrating oil, 23
Pivot bolts, 32, 46, 47, 50, 51, 198
Pliers, 22
Plunk-plunking in lowest gear, 146
Power train, 143–211. *See also specific
        parts.*
Pressure, tire, 111–112
Presta valve on tire, 96, 111–112
Problems, described, 11
Pumps, 19–20, 112–113
Puncture, in tire, 94–110
Putting wheel on bike, 108–110

Q

Quick-release lever, 97, 108–110
    replacing wheel with, 108–110
    on brake, 34
    on seat, 137, 139

R

R (Road Bike), viii
Racing bikes, 6
Rear changer, 208–211
    adjusting, 188–195
    chain throwing, 207–208
    loose chain and, 173
    noise from, 145, 146
    replacing, 210
    stickies in, 196
Rear sprocket (cog), 179–185
    noises from, 145
    replacing, 181–185
Rear wheel. *See also* Wheels.
    adjusting bearings (cruiser), 120
    removing, 97–98
    replacing, 108–110
    rubbing on frame, 114
Relativity, 4
Remover, crank, 26, 158
Removing a tire, 98–100
Removing a wheel, 97–98
Replacing parts. *See specific parts.*
Retention plate, pedal, loose, 153
Riding position, 3
Right and left on a bike, 9
Rim strip, 102
Rims, 93, 121. *See also* Spokes
        and rims.
Ritchey multi-tool, 21
Road bikes, viii, *See all* **R** paragraphs.
Rubbing
    of gear changer on chain, 206
    of tire on frame, 114
Rules of Thumb, 9–13
Rust-frozen parts, 11

S

Saddle. *See* Seat.
Schraeder valve, 96
Screwdriver, 16
Seat, 135–141
    loose, 137
    positioning, 137–140
    stealing of, 137
    swiveling, 137–139
Seat post, 135–141
Seat tube, 85
Secondary anchor bolt, 46
Set race, 84
Sew-up (tubular) tires, 7
Shifters. *See* Control levers (gears).
Shims
    handlebar, 69
    seat post, 139
Shocks, 5, 90
Shoes, brake, 54–57
    cockeyed, 54–55
    dragging, 49–51
    slipping when wet, 55
    squeaking, 57
    stickies in, 52
    worn, 55–56
Side-pull (caliper) brakes, 48
SIS systems, fine tuning, 194
Slippage. *See also* Looseness.
    in brakes when wet, 55
    in control levers, 202
    in gears, 145, 186, 202
Spanner, for hub work, 23
SPD. *See* Pedals.
Spokes and rims, 93–94, 121–134
    broken spokes, 132–134
    spare spokes, 26
    wobbling wheel and, 121–134
Spoke wrench, 23, 127–132
Sprocket noises, 148, 164. *See also*
        Front sprocket (chainring),
        Rear sprocket (cog).
Squeaking
    brake shoes, 57

Squeaking, *continued*
    in chain, 171–172
    from loose cranks, 148, 154
    in pedals, 149
Stem, 67–76
    handlebars loose in, 69
    loose or cockeyed, 69–71
    replacing, 71–72
Stickies
    in brakes, 30–31
        cable, 204–206
        hand lever, 31, 32–34
        shoes, 52
    in gear system
        cable, 204–206
        in control levers, 200–203
        in rear changer, 196
    in headset, 81–82
Stripped pedals, 151
Suckage, chain, 172
Swiveling seat, 137–139

T

Tape, replacing, 74
Tension, spoke, 127–129
Theft prevention, seat, 137
Third hand tool, 25–26
Thirty-day checkup, 8
Threaded parts, 10
Threadless headset, 77, 79, 81
Throwing chain, 169
    from front changer, 207
    from rear changer, 209
Thumb trigger (for gears), 197, 202
Tightness
    in bottom bracket, 160–161
    in chain, 174–176
    in headset, 81–82
    in pedal, 149
Tip (bar end) shifters, 197, 202
Tire irons, 17, 98–100
Tire patch kit, 17

Tires, 93, 94–114
    checking, 15, 95, 111
    finding leak in, 95, 100–102
    flat, 94–110
    flat prevention, 111
    inflating, 111–114
    patching, 102–110
    pump, 19, 111–114
    punctured, 94–110
    removing, 98–100
    replacing, 106–108
    sew-ups (tubulars), 7
    valves. *See* Valves (tire).
Tools, 16–27
Topeak multi-tool, 21
Touring bikes, 5, 218
Transverse cable, brakes, 46
Trek wrenches, 23, 24
Trashmo, 1
Truing a wheel, 121–134
Tubes, tire, 18, 94–110
    checking for leaks, 95, 100–102
    patching, 102–110
Tubing, frame, 85
Tubular tires. *See* Sew-up (tubular)
    tires.
Turned-down (drop) handlebars, 67,
    73
Turning problems, 81–82

U

Ultra-light bikes, 6
Used bike, buying, 1

V

V-brake, 46–47
Valves (tire), 95–96
    checking, 95–96, 112–113
    removing from rim, 102–103
    tightening, 95–96
Vise grip, 22, 126

W

Washing bike, 12
WD-48. *See* Penetrating oil.
Wet brakes slipping, 55
Wheels, 93–134
    bearings, checking, 114
    hubs, 114
    in buying decision, 6
    loose, 114–121
    problems, and headset, 78
    quick-release lever on, 97,
        108–110
    removing, 96–98
    replacing, 108–110
    rubbing on frame, preventing, 109
    spokes and rims, 93–94, 121–134
    tires, 94–114
    wobbling (rim wobbles), 121–134
When and where to ride, 14
Wind resistance, 3–4
Wire brake/gear. *See* Cable(s).
Wobble
    in front sprocket, 167–168
    in seat, 137–139
    in wheel (rim), 121–134
Worn-out chain, 176
Wrenches, 16, 21, 22

Y

Y-socket tool, 24
Y Wrench (Allen), 18